State Tax Policy

Policy

A Political Perspective

THE URBAN INSTITUTE PRESS
Washington, D.C.

THE URBAN INSTITUTE PRESS
2100 M Street, N.W.
Washington, DC 20037

Library of Congress Cataloging-in-Publication Data

Brunori, David
    State tax policy : a political perspective / David Brunori.
        p.   cm.
    Includes bibliographical references and index.
    ISBN 0-87766-703-9 (pbk. : alk. paper)
    1. Taxation—United States—States. 2. Income tax—United States—States. 3. State governments—United States. I. Title.
    HJ2385 .B78 2001
    336.2'01373—dc21

                                                                    2001001900

Printed in the United States of America

THE URBAN INSTITUTE is a nonprofit policy research and educational organization established in Washington, D.C., in 1968. Its staff investigates the social and economic problems confronting the nation and evaluates the public and private means to alleviate them. The Institute disseminates its research findings through publications, its Web site, the media, seminars, and forums.

Through work that ranges from broad conceptual studies to administrative and technical assistance, Institute researchers contribute to the stock of knowledge available to guide decisionmaking in the public interest.

Conclusions or opinions expressed in Institute publications are those of the authors and do not necessarily reflect the views of officers or trustees of the Institute, advisory groups, or any organizations that provide financial support to the Institute.

Acknowledgments

I have been very lucky to have many people provide help and encouragement during the two years it has taken to complete this work. I owe a debt of gratitude to the anonymous reviewers who truly improved the book. The book was immeasurably better after they finished their work. Tom Field, president of Tax Analysts, provided the inspiration to write about fair, efficient, and effective state tax policy. No one has worked harder for those ideals than Tom. I was encouraged by the irrepressible Professor Richard Pomp, who cannot know the depth of his influence. Few people possess his knowledge of state taxation or his commitment to justice. The Urban Institute Press once again afforded me the opportunity to write about state taxation—a subject to which I have devoted my professional career. Blair Potter, Scott Forrey, Elizabeth Miranda, and Glenn Popson guided me through the process. I have never met people as dedicated to excellence as the Urban Institute Press staff. Finally, none of this would have been possible without my wife Elisse Brunori. I owe all success to her.

All errors and failings you may find in this book are mine.

To the one man I admired most,
my father Joseph Brunori

Contents

1

The Importance of
State Taxation

State tax systems are in trouble.

—Tax administrator at the
Multistate Tax Commission
annual meeting in 1999

The above assessment sums up the prevailing view on the condition of state taxes at the start of the 21st century. And this warning has been sounded before. The ability of existing tax systems to adequately finance state governments has been the subject of considerable debate and discussion over the past decade. Indeed, volumes have been written describing the serious problems facing state taxation (Brunori 1998; Murray and Fox 1997). Many of these works warn of an impending crisis (Gold 1986), question the viability, and in some cases the "survivability," of a particular tax (Fox 1998; Mikesell 1998; Pomp 1998), and suggest courses of action for saving the state tax system (Hellerstein 1998).

That scholars and policymakers have weighed in on the fragile condition of state taxation is not surprising. The state tax systems in use today, after all, were implemented more than a half-century ago. Their fundamental structure, however, has remained largely unchanged. The sales and personal income taxes, the two dominant sources of revenue available to the states, were developed during a different time to raise revenue in a vastly different economy. The sales and use tax began as a "temporary" revenue measure during the Great Depression. The personal income tax was implemented more than a generation before that. The other types of taxes levied by state governments (corporate income, excise, inheritance, and property) are just as old, or in some cases older than, the sales and use tax. In many respects, the tax systems used by state governments today reflect the economy of the 19th century more than that of the 21st century.

New Challenges for State Tax Systems

There is an old saying among tax lawyers that an old tax is a good tax. Unfortunately, the tax systems constructed by state governments in the past are often inadequate for raising revenue today. While state taxes have remained essentially unchanged, the economy has moved from a manufacturing base to one dominated by services and intellectual property. In this new economy, businesses, even small companies, no longer produce and sell products in one or in a few states, but throughout the nation and the world.

Most recently, the age of electronic commerce has revolutionized how people work, play, and communicate. The economy in which people primarily bought locally manufactured goods no longer exists. In today's high-technology, global economy, the ability to purchase services or products from anywhere in the world is just a few keystrokes away.

To be sure, states are still collecting revenue. The prosperity of the late 1990s has led to record budget surpluses in most states. But tax experts broadly agree that state tax systems are not as efficient as they should be. When the inevitable economic downturns occur, and they will, the existing tax structures will be hard-pressed to meet revenue needs.

Questions about the systems' efficiency are a pressing matter, as state taxes have never been as important as they are today. State governments are providing more public services than ever. In addition to providing traditional services (e.g., state police, prisons, higher education, and highway maintenance), states are providing many services once supplied and paid for almost exclusively by the federal and local governments. It is not surprising, then, that state governments have been raising unprecedented amounts of money.[1] This growth in the importance of state taxation largely reflects several political and economic developments.

Devolution of Responsibility to the State Level

Since the 1980s, the federal government has been steadily shifting more responsibilities to the states, a phenomenon that is commonly called "devolution" in academic circles. The states have been asked (or, in many cases, required) to administer and pay for many programs that traditionally were the responsibility of the federal government. Welfare, Medicare, Medicaid, and highway maintenance are a few examples in which the states have replaced the federal government as the administrative body responsible for providing services. Although the costs of assuming many of these programs have been offset by increased federal funding and protections against unfunded mandates, devolution has contributed significantly to the recent growth in state government budgets.

Along with this shift in responsibility, political pressure and a flood of legal challenges have prompted state governments to take on an increasingly greater share of the costs of public education. While the federal government was traditionally responsible for elementary and secondary education, state governments have paid a decidedly greater percentage of school finance costs over the past decade. Some states, such as Michigan, finance virtually all elementary and secondary education.

Two primary developments explain the increased state funding of public education. First, the property tax revolts of the late 1970s and early 1980s seriously curtailed the ability of local governments to raise revenue. Thus, many state governments were forced to provide additional financial assistance to local school districts laboring under tax limitations.

Second, and perhaps more significant, legal and political challenges to the constitutionality and fairness of how local governments fund schools became increasingly common in the 1970s and 1980s. Wealthier school districts with larger tax bases could provide more money for educating their students than could poorer school districts. In many states, the wide gap between per pupil spending by rich and poor school districts led to political protest and legal challenges. Many state supreme courts ordered their state governments to distribute school spending equally between rich and poor districts. No other development has burdened state budgets more than the shift in public education financing.

The Politics of Antitaxation

In addition to the pressures of shifting financial responsibilities, states have experienced what can be called the "politics of antitaxation." Since the late 1970s, a concerted effort to politicize, even demonize, taxation has been under way. This often-fervent antitax sentiment is evident at all levels of government. Antitax politics fueled the passage of Proposition 13 in California and spurred property tax revolts around the country. Presidential and congressional candidates from both parties began to use taxes as a central part of their campaigns. Tax cuts became a regular theme for gubernatorial and legislative candidates seeking election in virtually every state. These developments helped spawn the initiative and referendum movement, which has traditionally been dominated by antitax crusaders (Brunori 1999). The politics of antitaxation have limited state governments' ability to raise revenue precisely when the demand for services and education spending has increased. This paradox has forced state revenue departments to squeeze more from the existing tax laws. State revenue departments have by all accounts become more aggressive in their audit and litigation efforts. This vigilance, in turn, has led businesses to increase spending on state tax lawyers and accountants for auditing as well as for planning purposes.

Another reason for the increased importance (from both the taxpayers' and the government's perspectives) in state and local taxation is that many corporations now pay more in combined state and local taxes than in federal taxes. This trend began in 1981, when for the first time many corporations paid greater state corporate income taxes than federal income taxes. And the trend has continued throughout the 1980s and 1990s. As a result, the business community is spending more resources on lobbying, auditing, planning, and litigating state tax issues (Pomp 1998). The increased attention to state taxation by the business community is illustrated by the often-contentious debates over the taxability of electronic commerce, corporate profits, and business inputs.

Concern with Economic Development

State tax policy has also grown in importance because of its use as an instrument to foster economic development. Over the past 25 years, state governments have engaged in wasteful competition against each other for business investment and jobs. In particular, political leaders have used their tax laws to encourage companies to relocate to (or to remain in) their states. The use of tax incentives to encourage economic activity generally violates the principles of sound tax policy (Brunori 1997). This interstate competition (well-documented in the academic and professional literature) has had undesirable effects. In addition to resulting in an ever-shrinking tax base, it has also provided an incentive for companies to pit states against each other in the endless quest for economic development and job growth.

The Continuing Importance of State Taxation

The political and economic pressures on state revenue systems have not changed the fundamental purpose of state taxation. State governments need revenue to fund the services sought by their constituents. This statement may appear obvious, but a surprising disconnect between providing public services and raising the revenue to pay for those services has plagued the government sector. The political rhetoric criticizing taxes and government spending masks a simple truth: Services cannot continue without proper funding. For example, even the most ardent antitax advocate would likely agree that roads must be constructed and repaired. Moreover, the majority of citizens would concur that state police officers and other essential government employees must be paid, and that important government services such as higher education must be funded. These obligations need to be met along with federal mandates, the challenges of devolution, and increased public-school financing responsibilities. Not surprisingly, given the importance of such services, the nation's legislators and governors have broad support for their efforts to ensure that state governments are adequately funded to meet the public's demands.

Just as citizens will continue to demand services, state governments—as they have throughout history—will need to find the revenue to pay for these programs. In the past, state political leaders have proved resourceful in financing government services despite the often significant political and economic challenges to state tax systems.

Thus, the question is not whether states will raise the necessary moneys, but from which groups the funds will be collected. State and local governments generally impose taxes on consumption, income, and property. Each of these tax categories has different effects on the various segments of society. Some taxes fall more heavily on the wealthy (progressive income taxes), while others fall more heavily on the poor (regressive sales and use taxes). In addition, some taxes are perceived to harm business and economic development (corporate income taxes).

Determining who bears the burden of paying for government is an important political question.

Public leaders face a difficult task: They must raise the requisite revenue, often by overcoming political opposition to taxes in general. In setting tax policy, they must weigh various concerns from constituents, business interests, and a myriad of organizations representing the poor, unions, and environmentalists. They must deal with issues of interstate competition, economic development, and tax relief for politically sympathetic groups such as veterans, the elderly, and children. While state taxation has never been more important, formulating state tax policy has never been more difficult.

A Look at State Tax Policy

The purpose of this book is to discuss the issues political leaders face when developing and implementing state tax policy. It will discuss the basic concepts of state taxation, including the theoretical underpinnings of policy and its real-world applications. This book will not turn the reader into an expert in state public finance; no single work can. Nor does it address every issue involved in state taxation. Again, no single work can accomplish that. Rather, the goal is to analyze the critical tax policy issues facing state governments. As described below, each of the chapters addresses a particular tax issue, the problems it has posed, and ideas on possible solutions in formulating and implementing state tax policy.

Tax Benchmarks

One of the most important questions facing state tax policymakers and political leaders is identifying the benchmarks against which the merits of a particular tax system can be measured. This question goes to the heart of what citizens, by electing particular officials, hope to achieve through their state tax laws.

Chapter 2 provides a discussion of what is widely referred to as "classic tax policy." Classic tax policy sets forth certain principles that can lead to viable revenue systems for all levels of government, including states. These principles, which hold that tax systems should be fair, efficient, stable, and accountable, have long been advocated by economists, political theorists, and state tax administrators.

Interstate Competition and Taxation

One of the greatest threats to a fair and efficient tax system is the inexorable quest for economic development. Chapter 3 addresses the relationship of economic development and its effect on the formation of state tax policy, a topic long debated in academic and policy circles. The chapter argues that state tax competition for economic development is a worthwhile public policy objective because it leads to innovation, experimentation, and efficiency. Such competition, however, must be conducted within a principled approach to ensure accountability. Interstate competition that aims to lower the burden for all taxpayers while ensuring the provision of necessary public services can have long-term, beneficial effects on a state's economy.

Significantly, chapter 3 also examines the less desirable forms of interstate tax competition that have proliferated over the past quarter-century—namely, targeted tax incentives aimed at particular industries or individual companies. The use of targeted tax incentives is portrayed as an unthinking response to the perceived political pressure to create jobs and spur economic development. The chapter concludes that targeted tax incentives violate the principles of sound tax policy.

Political Pitfalls

Chapter 4 explores the political interests that influence tax policymaking in the states. Tax policy plays a role in both electoral and legislative politics. It has been an integral part of state elections over the past quarter-century. Numerous governors and legislators have captured or lost public offices because of their position on how states should tax citizens. Virtually every election cycle features at least one statewide campaign in which taxes are the dominant issue.

Tax policy plays an even greater role in the legislative process. Business, public interest groups, labor, and education organizations routinely lobby state legislators on tax issues. The influence of large corporations (which employ many people), campaign contributors, and constituents on state tax policy is enormous.

Citizens, however, have also become an increasingly powerful force in the tax policy-making arena. Nearly half the states allow citizens to initiate and directly vote on tax policy issues. Over the past 25 years, policymakers have increasingly used this practice, known as direct democracy, to set tax policy. In the 1990s alone, citizens were asked to vote on more than 150 tax-related issues. And the number of tax-related ballot issues increases every year. The use of the initiative and referendum process to set tax policy raises many questions for state governments. In particular, should state tax policy be determined through a popular vote? Do citizens possess enough information to make educated decisions? Are tax-related initiatives more vulnerable to the demands of special interests than are tax policies set by legislation? As chapter 4 indicates, the implications of such initiatives for state governments are far-reaching.

Pressure on State Taxes

Beginning with chapter 5, the book examines policy issues presented by specific types of taxes. Although the analysis provides some information on the policy design of these taxes, the focus is on the economic, political, and social issues that arise in levying these particular taxes.

SALES AND USE TAX. Chapter 5 reviews one of the mainstays of state revenue systems, the sales and use tax. An important component of most state tax systems for more than a half-century, the sales and use tax accounts for nearly one-third of state tax revenue. In today's demanding economy, however, the sales tax is under intense pressure.

In 1998, for the first time since the Great Depression, the personal income tax replaced the sales tax as the single most important source of revenue for the states. The continuing pressure on the sales tax is the result of electronic commerce, the shift to a service-based economy, and the political pressure to exempt broad categories of products traditionally considered taxable. Many observers also view the sales and use tax as the most unfair of all state taxes.

PERSONAL INCOME TAX. Another important source of revenue is the personal income tax, which accounts for about one-third of state tax revenue. Unlike the sales and use tax, which is under constant pressure, the personal income tax is enjoying unprecedented growth. It also has widespread public support. The personal income tax raises a tremendous amount of revenue and is perceived by many to be the fairest of all state levies. Nonetheless, imposing state personal income taxes raises several important policy issues.

CORPORATE INCOME TAX. Chapter 7 looks at the corporate income tax, perhaps the most controversial of the state taxes. The corporate income tax accounts for less than 6 percent of state tax revenue. State governments and taxpayers, however, spend large amounts of resources administering and complying with the tax. Although experts cite several important reasons for taxing corporate income, the tax has continued to shrink as a source of revenue. This decline is due in part to an increase in the number of professionals dedicated to tax law and a greater amount of advanced planning by businesses to avoid corporate tax liabilities. It can also be attributed to the significant political pressure for states to grant tax breaks to corporations. Several factors—including the relatively small amount of revenue collected, the considerable cost of collecting the revenue, and the draconian steps required to revive the tax—have led many to question its long-term viability.

OTHER STATE TAXES. Chapter 8 describes the other categories of taxes imposed by states. Of these categories, state property taxes and death taxes generate very little revenue (less than 5 percent of total state revenue). Yet these taxes consume considerable compliance and administrative resources. In addition, they often create political problems for elected leaders.

Specialized excise taxes, one of the oldest sources of state revenue, account for approximately 20 percent of total state tax revenue. Many economic and political questions surround the use of various excises. Unlike income and sales taxes, excise taxes can promote social policy objectives while raising substantial revenue. For example, excise taxes on alcohol and tobacco could limit consumption of those substances. Excise taxes at the gas pumps will likely encourage fuel conservation. These kinds of social policy objectives, however, conflict with the notion that taxation should have a neutral effect on the market. These taxes are also widely regarded as regressive and seen to offer little potential for sustained revenue growth.

NONTAX REVENUE SOURCES. The states collect only about 40 percent of their total revenue through taxes. As explained in chapter 9, the nontax revenue sources used by state governments include intergovernmental aid; lottery revenue; fees and licenses; seizure of unclaimed property; and, increasingly, litigation activities. These sources of nontax revenue are important to discussions of tax policy. The availability of such revenue enables states to devise short-term funding strategies as they consider ways to address the problems facing their tax systems. For example, they can postpone implementing the politically difficult measures that are necessary to strengthen consumption and business taxes. But as discussed in chapter 9, the states' ability to rely on alternative revenue sources is inherently limited.

Challenges Ahead

The concluding chapter addresses the policy issues presented by the two most important economic developments since the Industrial Revolution: the globalization of markets and the advent of the age of electronic commerce. Together, these developments will continue to affect all aspects of society. State policy and political leaders are well aware of the threats presented by the new economy to their revenue systems. The state governments have already lost considerable tax revenue as a result of electronic commerce; they could lose much more.

Less well understood are the effects of international trade and global commerce on tax systems. The removal of governmental trade barriers, the mobility of capital, and the expansion of emerging economies will continue to hasten the growth of global trade. National borders will cease to be relevant. This increase in global trade will challenge state taxation systems in unprecedented ways. For example, international trade agreements may limit state taxation of foreign commerce, particularly corporate taxes. In addition, the rapid flow of goods across borders and the mobility of capital will make identifying the source of transactions and, thus, sales and income taxes, more difficult. The mobility of world capital will also increase pressure on the states to compete not only with other states but also with foreign national governments.

Chapter 10 contains five commonsense policy recommendations for states to consider as they address the issues facing their beleaguered tax systems. These policy recommendations do not involve significant tax reform or large costs. Although substantial tax reform may ultimately be necessary, these modest policy recommendations offer legislators and policymakers a broad framework for considering state tax policy. These policy recommendations can be implemented without cost or controversy and could help lead to more effective, and more equitable, state tax systems.

NOTE

1. A dramatic growth in state tax practices has accompanied the shift in revenue and services responsibilities to the states. Over the past 20 years, the number of tax lawyers and accountants in the private and public sectors has grown dramatically (Brunori 1997).

REFERENCES

Brunori, David. 1997. "Behind the Curve: State and Local Taxation in U.S. Law Schools." *State Tax Notes* (May 5): 1405–1408.

———. 1997. "Principles of Tax Policy and Targeted Tax Incentives." *State and Local Government Review* 29 (1): 50–61.

———. 1998. *The Future of State Taxation.* Washington, D.C.: Urban Institute Press.

———. 1999. "Initiatives and Referendums Are Here to Stay." *State Tax Notes* (May 17): 1635–1637.

Fox, William. 1998. "Can the State Sales Tax Survive a Future Like Its Past?" In *The Future of State Taxation,* edited by David Brunori (33–48). Washington, D.C.: Urban Institute Press.

Gold, Steven. 1986. "State Tax Policy." In *Reforming State Tax Systems,* edited by Steven Gold. Washington, D.C.: National Conference of State Legislators.

Hellerstein, Walter. 1998. "Electronic Commerce and the Future of State Taxation." In *The Future of State Taxation,* edited by David Brunori (207–223). Washington, D.C.: Urban Institute Press.

Mikesell, John. 1998. "The Future of American Sales and Use Taxation." In *The Future of State Taxation,* edited by David Brunori (15–32). Washington, D.C.: Urban Institute Press.

Murray, Matthew, and William Fox, eds. 1997. *The Sales Tax in the 21st Century.* Westport, Conn.: Praeger.

Pomp, Richard. 1998. "The Future of the State Corporate Income Tax: Reflections (and Confessions) of a Tax Lawyer." In *The Future of State Taxation,* edited by David Brunori (49–72). Washington, D.C.: Urban Institute Press.

2

Principles of Sound Tax Policy

Adam Smith? How many jobs can he create in Virginia?

—Legislator when told that a tax incentive plan would run
counter to the teachings of Adam Smith

Everyone wants to enjoy the benefits of "good" tax policy. But what constitutes good tax policy is often in the eyes of the beholder. To some individuals, good tax policy is measured by the burdens placed on individuals by the tax system; that is, what segments of the population should be responsible for paying particular shares of government costs. This question has sparked the seemingly endless debate of whether that responsibility should fall largely on the wealthy rather than on the less fortunate.

Others evaluate tax policy in terms of how it affects commerce and industry—whether the policy sparks or inhibits economic growth. But, as in the debate on what groups should be taxed more heavily, a great divide separates those who believe that the business community should be relatively unburdened and those who believe that businesses, rather than individuals, should pay for a greater share of public services.

For some, good tax policy depends on its political ramifications. For example, will a particular plan help constituents? Will it garner campaign contributions? Tax policy choices often lead politicians to ask the simple question: Will this course of action lead to reelection or certain defeat?

For still others, good tax policy is a function of one's philosophical views on the size and role of government and the wisdom of redistribution. Some believe that good tax policy is best determined by how effectively the government raises revenue for public services. Individuals with this viewpoint often think that how government raises revenue is less important than ensuring that funds are available to pay for government programs. Conversely, some individuals cast a wary eye on most government programs. Those with this kind of jaundiced view of the public sector tend to see taxes as a necessary evil—no matter how the government collects them.

All along this continuum are people who sincerely believe that their normative vision of good tax policy is in the best interests of society. Despite often wide-ranging ideological differences, much of the public debate over how the government should raise revenue takes place among people who are interested in developing tax policies that will benefit the country.

Of course, there will always be those individuals who have a much more cynical interest in advocating particular tax policy choices. These people view tax policy from a narrow, self-serving perspective and define good tax policy as whatever benefits their particular interests. But if one takes the more public-spirited approach, it is possible to develop a set of principles upon which large segments of society can agree.

The question of what constitutes sound tax policy has been debated for hundreds of years. Adam Smith was the first to articulate a set of guidelines for raising revenue in a market-based economy. In 1776, Smith enumerated four principles for evaluating a revenue system.

1. The subjects of every state ought to contribute toward the support of government, as nearly as possible, in proportion to their respective abilities; that is, in proportion to the revenue which they respectively enjoy under the protection of the state.
2. The tax that each individual is bound to pay ought to be certain and not arbitrary.
3. Every tax ought to be levied at the time, or in the manner, in which it is most likely to be convenient for the contributor to pay.
4. Every tax ought to be so contrived as both to take out and to keep out of the pockets of the people as little as possible, over and above what it brings into the public treasury of the state (Papke 1993, 386).

Smith's views have been echoed by scholars, policymakers, and practitioners for over two centuries (Blough 1955; Break and Pechman 1975;

Reese 1980; Shoup 1937). While applicable to tax systems at all levels of government, his views have become particularly important in the field of state taxation.

In the area of state taxation, two organizations—the National Conference of State Legislatures (NCSL) and the Lincoln Institute of Land Policy—have provided what is perhaps the best set of principles for sound tax policy. In 1988, those organizations gathered a group of lawmakers and academics to discuss improving state tax systems. The outcome of that meeting was the seminal report, "Principles of a High-Quality State Revenue System." The principles outlined in the report restate most tax theorists' beliefs about what constitutes a sound tax system. The report was widely circulated by NCSL in 1992, and it appeared in a much-cited book, *The Unfinished Agenda for State Tax Reform* (Gold 1988).[1]

Although policymakers and tax specialists continue to debate the particulars of good state tax policy, they generally agree on five broad principles.

Principle One: Provision of Appropriate Revenues

The primary purpose of any tax system is to raise revenue to cover the costs of public expenditures. The tax system, then, is merely a means (collection) to an end (funding outlays determined through the political process) (Blough 1955). This principle is particularly important in the state tax arena. As discussed below, balanced budget laws largely prevent states from deficit spending. Thus, the tax system must raise the requisite revenue to pay for those services that the public demands.

A tax system must not only provide for current spending, but also meet the future revenue needs of the state. In its widely circulated report, NCSL asserted that to meet the revenue needs of a state, a tax system must demonstrate sufficiency, stability, and certainty (NCSL 1992, 7).

Sufficiency requires that enough revenue be available to balance the state budget and to adapt that budget to changes in state spending. More broadly, the state tax system must be designed to raise enough revenue to fund the programs and policies demanded by the citizens and enacted by their elected representatives. The hallmark of sufficiency is that state tax systems maintain flexibility. Spending needs will vary over time as political and economic developments unfold.

Stability requires that a consistent amount of revenue be collected over time, necessitating a mix of taxes, "with some responding less sharply to economic change" than others (NCSL 1992, 7). For example, personal income taxes are widely thought to produce more revenue than other types of levies during economic expansions but not during recessions. By contrast, revenue raised through broad-based sales taxes tend to be relatively consistent during economic swings. Stability is important because most public services are designed to last for an indeterminate time. That is, much of what state governments spend money on (e.g., schools, roads, prisons) remains the same from year to year.

Certainty requires that policymakers keep the number and types of tax changes to a minimum. The 1992 NCSL report recognized that frequent changes interfere with economic choices and with long-term financial planning for both businesses and individuals. Frequent changes in the law also lead to increased compliance and administrative costs.[2]

Of course, all governments must recognize that in certain instances the revenue system must be altered to meet the needs of a changing economy or to improve fairness and efficiency. But most would agree that significant changes to state revenue systems should be implemented cautiously and with much forethought.

According to this first principle—raising adequate amounts of revenue to pay for existing and future public services—state governments have generally been successful. State public-finance systems have been remarkably adept at raising revenue through good and bad economic times.

Part of the states' success in raising sufficient revenue is attributable to the balanced budget requirements that essentially preclude states from deficit spending. The constitutions of 24 states require that the final state budget be in balance. In eight additional states, a balanced budget is a statutory requirement. And all states except Vermont have some legal requirement that a balanced budget be submitted by the governor or approved by the legislature. Thus, political leaders are often forced to make difficult choices between public services and the tax burdens that these services produce.

The states' success also reflects the political will of the legislative leaders who have found ways to pay for public services despite continuing economic and political challenges to raising tax revenue. This aspect of state politics has not been studied and is little understood by academics or the public. Yet legislatures, to their credit, have been remarkably resourceful in raising revenue through the most trying times. For the past quarter-century, state lawmakers have been able to provide the services demanded by their constituents in an atmosphere plagued by balanced budget laws, a shrinking tax base, and decidedly antitax political sentiments. The resourcefulness of lawmakers in funding state services under often-trying conditions is an underappreciated attribute.

But much of the success in funding government is due to the structure of the state tax systems themselves. As noted, these systems have proved quite capable of dealing with the public's service demands through both prosperous and lean times. A majority of the states' revenues have come from a mix of income and consumption taxes. The growth and stability of these levies have helped states weather economic cycles without significantly reducing public services.

The reliance on various types of taxes and sources of revenue has also provided extraordinary flexibility and discretion to state legislators. State lawmakers have been able to target (or otherwise limit) revenue reductions or increases to a particular tax. Thus, states have been able to raise revenue or cut taxes without significantly reforming the public finance system.

That the states have dealt so well in an ever-changing economic environment is surprising given that most major state tax systems were developed in the early 20th century. The country's economy at that time hinged on the manufacture of tangible personal property and farming. Over the past century, the U.S. economy has shifted to a service base and a greater dependence on international trade. Today, the age of electronic commerce is producing another dramatic economic shift.

So far, through all the economic changes, the state tax systems have managed to produce the revenue necessary to pay for public services. Whether or not they will continue to meet this objective is debated widely in public finance circles.

Principle Two: Neutrality

Most economists and political theorists agree that taxes should have as little an effect on market decisions as possible. Neither businesses nor individuals should be forced (or encouraged) to take action solely because of tax consequences, either positive or negative. Market conditions and economic efficiency—and not the tax code—should dictate business decisions. Similarly, taxes should not be used to influence individual consumption choices. To be sure, all taxes affect decisionmaking to some extent. Optimally, however, the tax system should minimize market distortions.

Policymakers widely agree that tax neutrality is best attained by a system with a broad tax base (i.e., one that has few exemptions, deductions, and credits) and low rates (NCSL 1992).[3] Tax systems built on a foundation of broad bases and low rates will minimize the opportunity and incentive to make economic decisions based on tax savings. Moreover, if the state must differentiate between groups of people in determining tax burdens, those differentials should reflect the external costs or transaction costs created by the taxpayers who bear the greatest burdens (Pogue 1998).

State tax systems have generally failed to attain neutrality. A host of tax provisions are designed to influence individual and business behavior. Literally thousands of provisions are on the books—far too many to discuss in one work. Businesses are provided deductions, credits, and exemptions as incentives to invest in plants and equipment and to expand their workforces. While these incentives are sometimes offered to all businesses in the state, in some cases they are offered to particular industries or specific companies. The incentives usually involve reductions in corporate income, sales and use, and/or property taxes. Government policymakers typically use these various tax incentives to motivate businesses to take actions that they believe the businesses would not otherwise take.

Individuals are granted tax breaks as well. Through the various state tax systems, people are encouraged to serve in the military, have children, own a home, attend college, and engage in other activities that they might not have undertaken but for the tax rewards involved. In addition, individuals' shopping patterns—where and when they make purchases—are influenced by sales-tax "holidays," exemptions for clothing, and exemptions on food for home consumption. Most people agree that the activities encouraged by individual tax breaks are socially desirable and should be promoted by the government. The question is whether the tax system is the most efficient way to accomplish these social goals.

It's important to note that individual and business behavior is influenced not only by tax breaks, but also by tax burdens. Tobacco and alcohol excise taxes are designed in part to discourage the use of these two substances by individuals. Moreover, corporate tax plans are often designed to encourage businesses to adopt policies that prevent pollution or help clean up the environment.

These examples show that the goal of neutrality is rarely met by state tax systems. The political and economic pressures inherent in a federal tax system, as discussed more fully in chapter 3, make achieving tax neutrality very difficult.

Principle Three: Fair and Equitable

Tax systems, like all aspects of government, should be fair and equitable. But the way to achieve equity through policy choices, perhaps more than any other aspect of sound tax policy, is subject to substantial disagreement. After all, "equity" is a concept fraught with value judgments, and fairness and justice are inherently difficult ideals upon which to build consensus. Furthermore, charges of inequity can be politically powerful. Political leaders routinely assert the unfairness of the revenue code when advocating tax policy. These cries of unfairness are not heard merely from "liberal" politicians crusading for the downtrodden; such rhetoric is just as likely to come from politicians representing the interests of wealthy corporations.

Despite these difficulties, tax experts have agreed on two general concepts of equity. In the tax policy realm, fairness is traditionally defined in terms of horizontal and vertical equity (Reese 1980).

Horizontal Equity

The concept that a tax system should treat similarly situated taxpayers the same is known as horizontal equity. Simply put, persons and businesses with similar incomes and assets should be taxed alike. This concept is closely related to the issue of neutrality discussed earlier. But while neutrality primarily concerns economic efficiency, horizontal equity—that people and firms should be treated equally—is seen as imperative in a democratic society.

Real or perceived differences in the taxation of equals undermine public confidence in a tax system. Consider a homeowner who discovers that his neighbor, with essentially the same house, pays substantially less in property taxes, or an employee who sees a coworker earning the same salary being taxed at a different rate. Such situations can only breed distrust of the tax system and government in general.

Moreover, the creation of horizontal inequities invariably leads to a smaller tax base. As individuals, groups, or particular transactions are exempted from a tax, the base shrinks. And a shrinking tax base leads to higher tax rates for everyone not enjoying the exemption. If certain purchases, such as food for home consumption, are exempt from sales tax, the state will have to increase rates on other purchases to raise the same amount of revenue. In effect, the people not receiving the benefit subsidize those who do.

Policymakers widely agree that taxes should be horizontally equitable. In practice, however, horizontal equity is elusive at all levels of government. As in the examples above, literally thousands of similarly situated individuals and businesses are being treated differently by the tax laws of virtually every state. Despite equal income and economic assets, a citizen's status as a veteran, parent, senior citizen, or student will often result in more favorable tax treatment.

Businesses, of course, are rarely treated uniformly by the tax system. States often reward companies that have made new investments in plants and equipment but not companies that have already made such investments. Similarly, companies receive tax breaks for hiring specified numbers of employees, but existing companies that have already hired the requisite numbers of employees do not receive the same benefits. Moreover, businesses with similar operations, revenue, and size are often treated differently because of their choice of entity.

The horizontal inequities presented by the tax system have not given rise to widespread public dissatisfaction or political upheaval. Part of the public's benign reaction is due to its general agreement that some of the groups receiving preferential treatment (e.g., veterans) deserve it. But some of the reaction, or lack thereof, reflects the public's limited knowledge about the consequences of creating horizontal inequities (greater tax burdens on everyone else) or even that these inequities exist.

Vertical Equity

Tax experts generally agree that the tax system should also be based, to some extent, on one's ability to pay. This much more politically problematic concept is known as vertical equity. Some observers argue that vertical equity requires a "progressive" form of taxation; that is, taxpayers should bear a greater burden of paying for government services as their income grows. Progressive taxes, depending on their design, could include corporate and business taxes; inheritance, estate, and gift taxes; property taxes; and individual income taxes. Others argue that equity requires a proportional form of taxation where all persons are taxed at the same rate. These individuals contend that most modern state taxes could be designed to impose a roughly proportional burden on all taxpayers.

A virtually undisputed notion, however, is that a sound revenue system minimizes regressivity (NCSL 1992). Regressivity means that a person's relative tax burden increases as his or her income or wealth decreases. Scholars, policymakers, political leaders, and most commentators writing on the subject of tax policy consider a regressive system unfair.

Although this consensus largely exists in academia[4] and among commentators, state tax systems have been decidedly regressive throughout their history (Citizens for Tax Justice 1996; Pechman 1985; Phares 1980).[5] In virtually every state, the poorer an individual is, the greater the percentage of his or her income that is paid to support the government. And in recent years, state taxes have become more regressive (Johnson and Lav 1997).

The regressive nature of state revenue systems is largely the result of the heavy reliance on consumption taxes (both general sales and use and excises).[6] As explained in detail in chapter 5, consumption taxes are regressive primarily because low-income individuals spend a larger percentage of their income on goods subject to tax than do high-income individuals. For example, sales taxes are generally not imposed on services; the wealthy spend a far greater percentage of their income on services than do the poor.

The effects of consumption taxes on the poor are somewhat offset by the personal income taxes levied in 41 states and the District of Columbia. But this progressive form of state taxation is not enough to overcome the regressive effects of the significant reliance on consumption taxes. General sales taxes are imposed by 45 states and have historically accounted for a third of state tax revenue. The various excise taxes account for about 20 percent of total state tax revenue. The states, therefore, rely on regressive levies for about half their tax revenue. (See chapter 5 for an in-depth discussion of sales and use taxes.)

Moreover, the majority of personal income tax systems are only mildly progressive. Most states have low rates and relatively few designated brackets. Several of the largest states (Texas and Florida, for example) do not tax personal income. As discussed in later chapters, the other taxes that could be considered progressive—corporate income and inheritance taxes—make up a very small percentage of total state tax revenue.

Making state tax systems more progressive, or at least less regressive, is a difficult, if not impossible, task. Consumption taxes are an important part of state public finance systems. They raise billions of dollars in revenue and cannot be replaced easily. Consumption taxes also have positive attributes that many believe may outweigh the problems of regressivity. Unfortunately, real and perceived problems associated with interstate competition prevent the states from significantly increasing their reliance on business and income taxes.

Thus, the states face a real dilemma. They rely heavily on regressive taxes, which are unfair, but political and economic conditions make reducing that reliance nearly impossible.[7]

State policymakers have been unable to devise a tax system that is either horizontally or vertically equitable. Given the tax system's impact on the poorest Americans, this inability is arguably the biggest failure of state tax policy.

Principle Four: Easy and Economical to Administer

The administrative requirements of sound tax policy entail minimizing the costs of compliance for taxpayers and of collection for the government (Reese 1980; Shoup 1937). If a revenue system is efficient it avoids complex provisions and regulations; multiple filing and reporting requirements; and numerous deductions, exclusions, and exemptions. In this sense, the need for simplicity is related to the goal of neutrality, because the factors that lead to complexity inevitably distort market decisions.

The more complicated the tax system grows, the greater the costs of taxpayer compliance. Both businesses and individuals will spend more time and money determining the requirements of the law and planning to minimize their tax burdens. Because a complicated tax system creates doubt as to the meaning of the law, both individuals and businesses will also spend more time and money defending against government audit activity as well as on litigation. Moreover, complexity often deters effective fiscal planning. Conversely, a less-complicated system of taxation facilitates understanding of the law and enhances public confidence in the system.

The government faces many of the same problems as individuals when navigating a complicated revenue system. From the government's perspective, complexity increases the costs of administration. The more complicated a system becomes, the more likely it is that taxpayers will express dissatisfaction. Tax systems with numerous exemptions, deductions, and credits require more audit and litigation resources. Ultimately, the complications (which are usually the result of a desire to ease regressivity or to provide incentives) require significantly more resources and thus raise the costs of enforcement and collection.

By and large, state tax systems get high marks for administrative ease and efficiency for taxes paid by individuals. Both sales taxes and personal income taxes place relatively small compliance burdens on individual taxpayers and minimal enforcement burdens on state revenue departments. For example, an individual's compliance obligations with respect to sales taxes end at the time of purchase; no forms need to be filed, no records kept, no accountants consulted. Similarly, withholding requirements and widespread conformance to federal tax laws minimize the burdens of complying with individual income taxes.

That is not to say no complications exist. Indeed, some areas of state tax law are replete with byzantine rules. In addition, as noted in chapter 5, compliance with rules on the individual use tax is virtually nonexistent. Estate and inheritance taxes are barely understood by most citizens (Brunori 2000). Although compliance costs are much greater for these taxes, the taxes themselves constitute a very small percentage of total state tax revenue.

State taxation tends to be much more complicated for businesses than for individuals. The most difficult state tax in terms of compliance and administration is the corporate income tax, although it accounts for less than 6 percent of total tax revenue. The already complex rules governing multistate corporate taxation are further complicated by constant efforts on the part of the state legislatures to change the law to encourage economic development. Moreover, additional costs arise in deciphering the considerable federal statutory and constitutional limitations on state taxation of corporate income.

The sales and use tax also poses administrative and compliance problems for business, especially for firms engaged in multistate operations. In general, vendors must collect and remit the sales tax to the state. They must keep track of the legal requirements in various taxing jurisdictions and file returns on a quarterly or monthly basis. They must also keep extensive records in case of an audit.

The goal of simplicity requires constant vigilance. Political pressure to alleviate burdens on the poor creates numerous sales and personal income tax exemptions. Political pressure to spur economic development creates numerous exemptions, deductions, and credits for virtually all taxes paid by businesses. The more the state governments create tax breaks (for either individuals or business), the more they complicate the system. Tax breaks for individuals or business entities increase the costs of compliance with, and the administration of, the tax laws.

Principle Five: Accountability

Achieving accountability requires states to play several roles. First, the government must ensure that those charged with the administration and enforcement of the tax laws are performing their duties efficiently and fairly. Few things are more damaging to taxpayer morale than corrupt or ineffective collection.

Second, the government must enforce the laws. People and businesses must pay their outstanding taxes. And the government must demonstrate the means and political will to ensure the collection of those taxes. Each principle of sound tax policy discussed here requires the government to enforce the revenue laws. As many countries have discovered, lax tax enforcement leads to widespread tax evasion.

For the past quarter-century, state revenue departments have largely been free of serious or widespread corruption. By all accounts, the states have done an exemplary job of collecting revenue. Most revenue departments receive high marks for their professionalism and effectiveness.

The third aspect of accountability—open, transparent tax policy— has proved more difficult for states to achieve. In a democratic society, tax decisions should be made openly, and the laws governing taxes should be explicit rather than hidden. The costs and benefits of fiscal decisions, especially those that favor particular taxpayers, should be understood by the electorate as well as by tax administrators. Accordingly, government information regarding the tax system, including all documents that promulgate tax policy, should be open to the public for review. Only through open government decisionmaking can the public determine whether elected officials are adequately serving the public's interests.

Nonetheless, much state tax policy is being developed and implemented behind closed doors at both the legislative and executive levels of government. The legislative secrecy that often surrounds tax law is nothing new; it has occurred for years. Typically, a person, corporation, or industry will lobby a legislator for a particular tax benefit. For various reasons, the entity or legislator may not want the particular tax benefit to become public knowledge.[8] In many case, the legislator will then attempt to "hide" the true beneficiary by burying the proposed change in legislation that appears to have general applicability.

Literally hundreds of attempts to affect tax law in this way occur every legislative session. Most of these efforts are unsuccessful; however, one recent case in which the legislator succeeded, and one in which the attempt almost succeeded, are worth noting. In 1999, the Virginia legislature passed a law creating a sales-tax exemption for certain purchases of computer equipment. Later research revealed that only one taxpayer—the Internet giant America Online (AOL)—would benefit from the exemption. The legislation was crafted so that it appeared to apply to all purchases of computer equipment; in reality, AOL alone was entitled to tax exemptions, amounting to $18 million. The most surprising aspect of the case was that most Virginia lawmakers did not realize the law benefited only one taxpayer (Brunori 1999).

In 1999, in a similar but ultimately unsuccessful bid, Maryland legislators proposed a law that would have capped income tax liability for capital gains at $104,000. At the time, most legislators and the public did not know that only one-tenth of 1 percent of the state's population would benefit from the measure. The press later reported that the legislation resulted from the lobbying efforts of a single wealthy individual (Brunori 1999). The legislation eventually failed, but few Maryland lawmakers realized that the benefits would apply to a small percentage of citizens.

Administrative secrecy is also a widespread phenomenon in state tax matters. Many laws either expressly or implicitly prevent public access to state administrative actions. Few would argue that sound tax policy requires confidential taxpayer information to be disclosed. Individuals' tax return information, and some businesses', should, as a general rule, not be disclosed to the public. But administrative documents that set tax policy should clearly reside in the public domain. Such documents, however, are not always available for review.

For example, in 1998, the Georgia legislature passed Georgia Code Sec. 48-7-31(d)(1). This statute allows corporate taxpayers that are planning to build new, or expand existing, facilities in Georgia to enter into an agreement with the state revenue commissioner on the allocation and apportionment of the corporation's revenue for corporate income tax purposes. To date, little or no published information is available on which companies have taken advantage of the law or the terms of any of the agreements. Nor is there a mechanism allowing the public or press to obtain this information (Kerner 2000).[9]

Finally, accountability requires states to review existing laws and determine whether they are serving the needs of the citizens. Only through periodic evaluations can the public and its elected representatives know if the policies are successful at raising revenue or if they are in need of revision. Such evaluations also help determine if a state's tax policies are fair. Moreover, tax policy that is meant to promote or deter specific behavior (such as economic investment) must be evaluated on whether it meets the intended goal.

Despite the importance of preserving the integrity of tax systems, most states score poorly on evaluating their laws and policies. Some states have established commissions to study tax reform needs (McGuire and Rio 1995). Few states, however, conduct routine evaluations of their revenue systems. For example, no state conducts incidence studies to determine who is paying what share of government services. And only a few states conduct these kinds of studies when considering legislation (Johnson and Lav 1997).

The states play no role in determining the regressivity of the tax laws. Similarly, no states conduct regular studies to determine whether the tax laws are raising revenue in an efficient and economical manner. In general, states have also not evaluated inefficient, costly, or burdensome rules and regulations governing compliance and administration. Moreover, the states fail to examine whether the myriad of tax laws are functioning the way they were intended. Does a particular tax raise enough revenue to justify the compliance and administrative costs? Does a particular tax or procedure no longer make sense because of changing economic conditions? These and similar questions are rarely addressed by the states except when an infrequent commission is established to conduct a comprehensive review of the finance system.[10] The reason that states fail to evaluate their revenue laws regularly is that they are not legally required to do so. State legislatures have not mandated (or appropriated funds for) such studies.

The Quest for Sound Tax Policy

The states receive mixed reviews on how well they comply with the established principles of sound tax policy. Tax systems are considerably less fair and more complicated than the ideals described here would mandate. At the same time, the systems have proved resilient to economic change and have consistently managed to produce enough revenue to keep public services funded. And tax enforcement is generally strong, although many aspects of state tax policy are steeped in secrecy.

Tax experts widely agree on what constitutes sound tax policy. But devising policies and government practices that adhere to these principles is much more difficult. Political and economic pressures can lead to laws and regulations that often conflict with the principles described here. Tax breaks for particular individuals or businesses, often made in the name of fairness or economic development, usually lead to less equitable, less neutral, and more costly tax systems. But such tax breaks will likely continue as long as political leaders lobby for their constituents' interests. Perhaps most troubling is the regressive nature of many tax policies. Although virtually every expert agrees that tax systems should minimize regressivity, the federal system and interstate competition for wealthy individuals and businesses have made regressivity almost inevitable.

Yet, the goals set forth in the principles are worth striving toward. It may be difficult to create a fair and efficient tax system, but the difficulty alone should not be a deterrent. Good government requires sound tax policy; it is incumbent upon our political leaders to pursue that ideal.

NOTES

1. Other works have brought together essays by leading thinkers in the field. For example, in Steven D. Gold's edited volume *Reforming State Tax Systems* (1986) many noted

tax scholars—among them Richard D. Pomp, Andrew Reschovsky, John Shannon, Robert P. Strauss, Thomas Pogue, and John L. Mikesell—opine on improving the methods used by states to collect taxes. That work remains a classic in the field.

2. Political rhetoric at times suggests that the tax profession favors uncertainty in taxation because it makes tax services more valuable. Only the most cynical, unprofessional tax practitioner would consider frequent changes to the tax structure a sound policy objective.

3. Low rates and broad bases have long been recognized as a goal of sound tax policy at all levels of government. Indeed, these two policy components were the cornerstone of the last significant federal tax reform effort, which culminated in the Tax Reform Act of 1986 (Steuerle 1992).

4. Although most economists and tax theorists agree that at least a small measure of progressivity is desirable, there are a few dissenters, such as Joseph (1996).

5. The degree of regressivity of state tax systems has been the subject of some debate (Reschovsky 1998).

6. Reschovsky (1998) notes that regressivity is also a result of political pressure, exerted by the wealthy, on state governments to reduce progressivity.

7. While attaining progressivity is difficult, the states could provide additional tax relief to the poor in a number of ways, including expanded deductions, exemptions, and refundable credits of various taxes (Gold and Liebschutz 1996).

8. Legislators prefer to keep their advocacy for government expenditures benefiting particular persons or corporations out of the media's view and off the political opposition's scorecard.

9. Another example worth mentioning is the Illinois Economic Development for a Growing Economy (EDGE) program, signed into law in April 1999. This law enables companies to apply for job-creation tax credits. The application and agreement, as well as the tax savings, are not in the public records (Smith 2000).

10. Even in those cases in which the law requires review and results can be measured relatively easily, most states fare poorly in evaluating their tax policies. For example, one recent study found that virtually no states have effectively evaluated whether tax incentives granted to corporations as a means of spurring economic development have actually accomplished their intended goal (Good Jobs First 2000).

REFERENCES

Blough, Roy. 1955. *The History and Philosophy of Taxation.* Williamsburg, Va.: College of William and Mary.

Break, George, and Joseph Pechman. 1975. *Federal Tax Reform.* Washington, D.C.: Brookings Institution.

Brunori, David. 1999. "Private Tax Relief and Secret Incentives." *State Tax Notes* (March 15): 1829–1830.

———. 2000. "Taxing Death and Other Happy Thoughts." *State Tax Notes* (April 7): 1369–1371.

Citizens for Tax Justice and the Institute on Taxation and Economic Policy. 1996. "Who Pays? A Distributional Analysis of the Tax Systems in All 50 States." *State Tax Notes* (July 29): 311.

Gold, Steven D., ed. 1986. *Reforming State Tax Systems*. Denver, Colo.: National Conference of State Legislatures.

————. 1988. *The Unfinished Agenda for State Tax Reform*. Denver, Colo.: National Conference of State Legislatures.

Gold, Steven D., and David S. Liebschutz. 1996. "State Tax Relief for the Poor." *State Tax Notes* (May 6): 1397–1404.

Good Jobs First. 2000. *Minding the Candy Store: State Audits of Economic Development*. Washington, D.C.: Institute on Taxation and Economic Policy.

Johnson, Nicholas, and Iris Lav. 1997. "Are State Taxes Becoming More Regressive?" *State Tax Notes* (October 6): 893–895.

Joseph, Richard, J. 1996. "Why Progressive Taxation?" *Tax Notes* (January 15): 313–318.

Kerner, Jessica. 2000. "Secret Agreements—Georgia Corporate Income Tax—Allocation and Apportionment." *State Tax Notes* (June 9): 2101–2103.

McGuire, Therese, and Jessica Rio. 1995. "Toward State Tax Reform: Lessons from State Tax Studies." *State Tax Notes* (November 27): 1543–1553.

National Conference of State Legislatures (NCSL). 1992. *Principles of a High-Quality State Revenue System*, 2d. ed. Washington, D.C.: NCSL.

Papke, James. 1993. "A Reexamination of the Indiana Tax Structure: Introduction and Overview." *State Tax Notes* (February 22): 386.

Pechman, J. A. 1985. *Who Paid the Taxes, 1966–1985?* Washington, D.C.: Brookings Institution Press.

Phares, Donald. 1980. *Who Pays State and Local Taxes?* Cambridge, Mass.: Oelgaschlager, Gunn, and Hain.

Pogue, Thomas. 1998. "State and Local Business Taxation, Principles, and Prospects." In *The Future of State Taxation*, edited by David Brunori (89–110). Washington, D.C.: Urban Institute Press.

Reese, Thomas. 1980. *The Politics of Taxation*. Westport, Conn.: Quorum Books.

Reschovsky, Andrew. 1998. "The Progressivity of State Tax Systems." In *The Future of State Taxation,* edited by David Brunori (161–190). Washington, D.C.: Urban Institute Press.

Shoup, Carl. 1937. *Facing the Tax Problem.* New York: Twentieth Century Fund.

Smith, Frances. 2000. "The Illinois EDGE Program: Low Accountability Despite Safeguards." *State Tax Notes* (July 3): 47–90.

Steuerle, C. Eugene. 1992. *The Tax Decade: How Taxes Came to Dominate the Public Agenda.* Washington, D.C.: Urban Institute Press.

3

Interstate Competition for Economic Development

If they're creating jobs, we will give them what they want.

—State legislator, when asked about the wisdom of
providing targeted tax relief to Fortune 500 companies

One of the most significant pressures on state tax policy is interstate competition for economic development. Throughout their history, U.S. state governments have competed for economic development in the form of investment and job creation.[1] Tax policy has played a large role in that competition. For much of the past quarter-century, political leaders have viewed state tax policy as the key to encouraging economic development. Tax benefits are used to lure corporations into a state or to convince corporations to stay. Taxes are also used to encourage in-state companies to expand through investment in plants and equipment as well as to encourage businesses to expand their workforces through additional hiring.

The role of taxation in interstate competition for economic development has been studied and debated for years, as demonstrated by the volumes written on virtually all aspects of competition among state and local governments (Kenyon and Kincaid 1991; Lynch 1996; Schweke, Rist, and Dabson 1994). Most of the literature has a decidedly negative tone about the effects of interstate tax competition on state taxation. According to many researchers, the policy choices that result from interstate tax competition violate one or more of the principles of sound tax policy discussed in chapter 2.

Three concepts are important to understanding interstate tax competition for economic development. First, interstate competition in

31

general, and tax competition in particular, is a fact of life in the United States. For hundreds of years, political leaders have implemented policies that they believe will benefit their citizens. The more attractive these policies seem, the more likely it is that citizens and business will remain in or locate to the state. As long as the states enjoy even a small amount of sovereignty over their public affairs, they will set policies that retain or attract people and business.

Second, not all forms of interstate competition are equal. Some types of competition are desirable because they promote innovation, efficiency, and responsiveness. Such desirable competition includes providing an attractive package of public services (presumably better than those offered in neighboring states), while imposing overall tax burdens aligned with those of other states. If competition is inevitable, as history suggests, state lawmakers are left to decide what form that competition should take.

Third, political bias is built into the most pernicious type of competition: targeted tax incentives. This form of competition involves granting tax breaks to individual companies to move to or to remain in a state. Such tax incentives, which are inequitable, inefficient, and largely unnecessary, violate virtually every principle of sound tax policy and good government. Public officials and academics alike routinely criticize targeted tax incentives, which have nonetheless proliferated in the past quarter-century.

Why States Compete

As noted, interstate competition, including interstate tax competition, is inevitable. The competition reflects the belief that government policy influences, at least to some degree, where people live and work. It also arises because individuals and businesses can assess the tax burdens and public services of other states and make choices accordingly. More broadly, interstate tax competition is driven by state sovereignty, a changing economy, and the political pressure to create jobs.

States as Sovereigns

The principal cause of the never-ending battle between the states' economies is the structure of the federal system of government. In essence, the states can govern as they wish within the limits imposed by the federal and state constitutions. Within this structure, states have the power to tax and to spend within very wide parameters. They have the power to decide whom to tax and whom not to tax, as well as what types of public services they should or should not provide. The sovereignty of the states also allows them to set policies that will make them more attractive to business and industry than other states. This environment stimulates competition.

Few outside factors limit the ability of a state government to tax and spend. As noted in chapter 4, political leaders have an interest in minimizing the tax burdens on their constituents while maintaining high levels of public services. Residents, businesses, and the press routinely evaluate governmental policies in part by how other states govern. These groups often judge political leaders by the tax burdens and public services profile of other states.

To some degree, the Commerce Clause of the U.S. Constitution prevents states from engaging in overaggressive competition, by ensuring that states do not impose tax burdens on out-of-state companies and transactions that are greater than the burdens placed on in-state companies and transactions. For example, a state cannot impose a sales tax on goods produced out of state if the law exempts similar goods produced within the state from being taxed. The Commerce Clause, however, does not prevent states from providing nondiscriminatory incentives to companies that conduct business or invest in the state. Historically, states have had virtually free reign in providing subsidies, including tax benefits, to in-state companies.[2]

The Changing Economy

The federal system itself gives rise to state tax competition for economic development. Other factors, however, also contribute to an atmosphere that virtually ensures such competition. After all, the federal system has existed for more than 225 years, but the use of tax incentives has increased dramatically only in the past quarter-century. Another factor increasing interstate competition is the changing world economy. In the not-too-distant past, most American businesses manufactured tangible personal property or produced agricultural products in one or a few states. At that time, capital was largely immobile, which meant that the means of production (e.g., factories and farms) could not be moved very easily from one state to another. Thus, while competition is evident as far back as the nation's start, the importance of attracting significant capital and investment did not surface until well into the 20th century.

The service industry has replaced manufacturing as the driver of the U.S. economy. The service industry relies far more on human capital and intangible property (e.g., copyrights, patents, and trademarks) than does the traditional manufacturing industry. The age of electronic commerce is further altering the business landscape as companies increasingly create, market, and sell goods and services through the Internet. Plants, equipment, and land—the inputs that are most difficult to move—are relatively minor components of today's booming electronic commerce.

An economy built on mobile capital and intangible property is subject to much greater interstate competition than a manufacturing-based economy. High-technology companies and service firms can relocate to other states at much less cost than can traditional manufacturing companies.

The Quixotic Quest for Jobs

Professor Richard Pomp of the University of Connecticut, an astute observer of interstate tax competition, has likened a state's quest for jobs to the search for the Holy Grail (Pomp 1998). The legend of the Holy Grail remains so compelling because the reward—eternal life—is so grand. Professor Pomp's analogy is an apt one: Government leaders are enthusiastic about tax incentives because the political payoff—jobs—is immensely attractive.

Interstate tax competition is largely about job creation, which is considered one of politicians' primary responsibilities. The methods of creating jobs, however, have changed. Not so long ago, one of the most powerful weapons a politician had was the ability to grant a constituent a job. These jobs usually fell within the government sector and were considered part of the patronage system. Occasionally, politicians could place people within well-connected businesses. Politicians often served as a key link between jobs and people.[3]

Today, civil service and government contract reforms have significantly curtailed the use of patronage to secure jobs. But the lure of creating jobs remains. One relatively quick way to create jobs is to provide incentives that draw established companies into the state. A long list of commentators note the relationship between the political pressure to create jobs and interstate tax competition (Spindler and Forrester 1993; Walker 1989; Wolman 1988).

A political leader's ability to create jobs through economic-development incentives is far greater than under the old patronage system. Unlike the patronage system, which contained inherent limits on the number of jobs a politician could create, a single incentive agreement can generate, or at least give the impression of generating, thousands of jobs. It is not surprising that job creation is an incentive to compete. Jobs have much to do with one's standard of living. The desire to earn a living, live comfortably, and take care of one's family are the real drivers of economic progress. And the importance of these factors is well understood by political leaders.

Despite the warnings about competition, not all interstate competition is undesirable. For example, most scholars view competition in overall state tax levels as positive. In this form of competition, states measure the attractiveness of their business climate by comparing their overall tax burden with that of surrounding states or of those seen as competitors for business development.

As noted in Duncan (1992), ensuring that one's state does not "stand out" from other states in terms of rates, burdens, or compliance costs promotes many aspects of sound tax policy. Such evaluation often leads to a balanced tax system, or at least protects against serious imbalances, and lends stability to the tax system. It can also help maintain the kind of broad-based, low-rate tax systems that are important to sound tax policy. In the most general terms, healthy interstate competition involves the use of various methods, including tax policy, to develop an attractive mix of public services at a reasonable cost to taxpayers. States must attract people and businesses by providing quality transportation, public safety, and education systems while keeping their tax burdens aligned with those of other states. Faced with resident migration, states cannot increase tax burdens substantially beyond those imposed by their neighbors (Musgrave 1959; Oates 1972).

John Shannon (1991), one of the leading thinkers on federalism and interstate competition, has noted that states competing against each other's tax profiles are like ships in a wartime convoy: They cannot risk getting too far ahead of their comrades by raising tax burdens, nor can they afford to fall too far behind in providing public services. Individuals and firms evaluate the costs (taxes) and benefits (services) of living or doing business in a jurisdiction. If the costs outweigh the benefits, then the individual or firm will opt to live or conduct business in a more favorable environment.

Most important, many public-finance experts (Duncan 1992) and political theorists (Kincaid 1991) accept, and even endorse, interstate competition in the area of overall tax burdens. These commentators believe that such competition promotes innovation, responsiveness, and efficiency. State competition in the area of overall tax burdens, however, can also have negative consequences because it often reduces the progressivity of state tax systems. If the theory of tax competition holds true, firms and households will reside in states where the public benefits outweigh tax costs. In general, as policymakers know, wealthier individuals and firms have greater means to relocate. To attract (or retain) wealthy firms and households, states often target their tax incentives and services to this group (Reschovsky 1998). Thus, tax liabilities for those on the top of the economic spectrum are held in check. At the same time, the public's demand for quality services must be met. Thus, interstate competition may place the greatest tax burden on those firms and households that are perceived as less likely to leave the jurisdiction. Still, this general type of interstate tax competition, despite its detrimental effects on tax equity, is far more attractive from a policy perspective than the alternative discussed below.

Targeted Tax Incentives: The Scourge of State Tax Policy

The most criticized, and pervasive, form of competition is the granting of targeted tax incentives to specific companies. Targeted tax incentives are laws that provide preferential tax treatment to a limited number of taxpayers and are not readily available to taxpayers in general. Such incentives offer special tax treatment to specific companies in return for business activity in the state. These incentives often include property tax abatements, sales and use tax exemptions, job and investment credits, and accelerated depreciation deductions.

Targeted tax incentives should not be confused with general tax policies that apply to broad segments of the business community. Targeted incentives specifically benefit a small number of corporations. The states providing the incentives want the recipients to locate to, expand within, or remain in the state.

Targeted tax incentives are often offered as part of a general revenue law that allows any business meeting certain requirements to qualify for the special tax status. Actually, however, these "general" statutes benefit only a few companies. For example, Virginia's major facility job tax credit enables individuals, estates, trusts, and corporations that engage in "qualifying industry" to receive an income tax credit of $1,000 for each new job created after 100 jobs (Virginia Code, sec. 58.1-439). Few small or midsized companies, however, can hope to generate that many jobs. In addition, the credits are only available to companies that announced expansions after January 1, 1994.

Targeted tax incentives have proliferated over the past quarter-century as states have stepped up efforts to spur economic development and job creation. Hundreds of such incentives are granted each year, costing taxpayers hundreds of millions of dollars.[4]

Despite a legion of scholarly articles and reports criticizing their use, targeted tax incentives remain a favorite weapon in the battle for economic development. Companies simply hint at the possibility of relocation or expansion, and state governments quickly offer to pay for infrastructure improvements, help with job training, and provide numerous tax breaks.

Why States Use Targeted Tax Incentives

States rely on targeted tax incentives partly because political leaders often perceive that other types of interstate competition, such as low tax rates and good services, do not work quickly enough. Targeted tax incentives are a relatively new and expedient way to create jobs. Many types of public services (transportation and education systems, in particular) often require years to develop or improve. Many state political leaders, however, do not want to wait to entice a corporation to locate to or expand within the state. As history illustrates, negotiations for and approval of tax incentives can be accomplished in a matter of months. Targeted tax incentives are linked inextricably to state political leaders' desire to move quickly in matters of economic development.

Moreover, once states show an interest in a company's business, the pressure to "strike first" mounts quickly; each state scrambles to offer an incentive package before a competitor can (Noto 1991). Interstate competition often results in an "arms-race" mentality. State governments feel the need to develop incentive strategies because other states are doing so.

Meanwhile, states with companies that are being lured away act defensively to ward off the challenge and to retain their industries (Grady 1987). Many states have a policy, usually implicit, to match or exceed offers of tax incentives offered to corporations by other states.

As noted by one important commentator, the need to create jobs and the negative appearance of "doing nothing" are simply too great for states *not* to engage in bidding wars (Duncan 1992, 269). Because of this fear of doing nothing, political leaders have essentially ignored the criticism of their reliance on these incentives. Tax policy, at least as far as targeted tax incentives are concerned, is often a matter of political expediency.

Policy Issues Raised by Targeted Tax Incentives

Targeted tax incentives violate all the principles of sound tax policy (Brunori 1997). Economists, political theorists, and commentators have all criticized the use of targeted tax incentives because they involve significant cost, violate principles of fairness, add to administrative inefficiency, and raise accountability questions.[5]

ADDED COSTS. The primary purpose of the tax code is to raise money. In addition to the political need to create jobs, the rationale often used to defend company-specific tax incentives is that the company receiving the incentives will eventually contribute more revenue than the state initially loses in granting the incentives. However, targeted tax incentives may end up costing the state more, since the state cannot guarantee that the expected economic windfall will follow a tax incentive deal.

Although research has looked at the effects of state tax policy on economic development (Bartik 1991), no studies by tax scholars or state policy analysts have examined the long-term effects of targeted tax incentives on state economies. More rigorous economic analysis is needed to measure the effectiveness of concessions granted to individual businesses (Noto 1991).

Targeted tax incentives may actually undermine a state's efforts to promote economic development by reducing a state's ability to produce adequate revenue and to provide necessary services—most likely key factors in location decisions (Bartik 1996; Lynch 1996). If states must reduce services, long-term economic growth could decline. Furthermore, when offering company-specific tax incentives, state governments often face greater infrastructure demands. For example, a new manufacturing facility employing several thousand workers may require additional government services such as roads, schools, and police and fire protection. These obligations, in turn, put pressure on the states to raise additional revenue.

South Carolina provides a recent illustration of the effects of this revenue pressure. In the 1990s, the state added about 200,000 new jobs. Many of these jobs, however, came from companies that had benefited from an estimated $2.7 billion in tax incentives provided by the state. Although thousands of new jobs were created, the state had problems funding ongoing public services and did not have enough revenue to fund long-term infrastructure and education projects (Hancock 1999).

Another criticism of targeted tax incentives is that they are generally offered to companies that would have undertaken the desired investment in any case. Two important studies (Vaughan 1979 and Harrison and Kanter 1978) and an abundance of anecdotal evidence support this criticism.[6]

There is little evidence that targeted tax incentives generate additional revenue for state government. For states that offer exceptionally large tax incentives, the prospect of recovering the forgone tax revenue is uncertain. Given the large amount of revenue involved and the added infrastructure costs, targeted tax incentives could end up costing the state money in the long run.

EQUITY. The biggest drawback of company-specific tax incentives is that they are fundamentally unfair. By design, they are neither horizontally nor vertically equitable. Usually, only the largest and most profitable companies are in a position to take advantage of targeted tax incentives. For example, in the 1990s, New York City provided more than $3 billion in tax incentives to 66 of the nation's largest corporations (Brunori 2000a). But those benefits did not extend to smaller businesses or individuals. A state that gives Fortune 500 companies substantial tax relief while subjecting small businesses to regular state taxes fails to distribute burdens equally. In Alabama, generous incentives will likely exempt Mercedes-Benz from state corporate income tax for 25 years (LeRoy 1994). The state's smaller companies will not have that kind of good fortune.

Small businesses are not the only ones who feel the sting of tax incentives granted to large corporations. Other taxpayers must make up for the lost revenue. In a recent study, the Louisiana Coalition for Tax Justice found that, over a 10-year period, just nine companies received half of the $2.5 billion in tax incentives provided by the state's Industrial Property Tax Exemption. In 1989, Louisiana's business property tax abatements totaled $273 million, a quarter of the state's total property-tax collection (Schweke, Rist, and Dabson 1994). Local governments depend on property taxes to fund basic services such as education and public safety. When the largest corporations are exempt from paying full property taxes, other property owners, particularly homeowners, end up financing a larger share of these services.

Unfortunately, no empirical work examines the distributional effects of targeted tax incentives. The consensus among experts, however, is that targeted tax incentives for industries and specific companies have a regressive effect on state tax systems. Removing these businesses from the tax rolls (while, in many cases, spending more money on infrastructure for these businesses) shrinks the tax base and increases government costs. With large businesses paying less taxes, the burden of paying for government is further shifted to individuals, with the wealthiest paying a proportionately smaller share of the costs. Furthermore, targeted tax incentives inevitably fail the test of horizontal equity because they do not treat similarly situated taxpayers equally. If company X receives preferential tax treatment for establishing a business in a particular community, what about company Y, which is already doing business in that community? For example, as noted, to obtain a tax credit in Virginia, the recipient must create more than 100 new jobs. Moreover, the credits are available only for expansions announced after January 1, 1994. What becomes of the company that already employs substantial numbers of people but is not in a position to expand by 100 employees? What becomes of the company that announced plans for expansion in 1993?

The inequity involved in providing some companies with incentives while denying them to other companies is spurring action in the business community (Brunori 2000b). Companies that want to stop their competitors from receiving specially designed incentives are lobbying state legislatures—successfully—for similar treatment. Given the states' revenue constraints, the increased demand for incentives could lead to a significant reduction in their use.

ADDED ADMINISTRATIVE INEFFICIENCY. Targeted tax incentives inevitably lead to more frequent changes in the tax laws. These changes, in turn, make administration of the revenue system more difficult and more expensive for both taxpayers and the government. As states sacrifice tax revenue to lure businesses, they need to find additional funds to pay for existing government services and additional infrastructure costs (Duncan 1988). Some states are likely to respond by expanding the tax base, further complicating their revenue systems. If targeted incentives lead to changes in rates, exemptions, and deductions, compliance costs for taxpayers will ultimately rise.

For state governments, the costs and complexity of administering the revenue system also increase (Duncan 1988). Substantial resources are required to enforce compliance and to explain the incentive structure to qualifying companies. The result is often "frustration for the tax department, the development agency, and the potential user taxpayer because of the uncertainty of the effect of a company incentive on business operation" (Duncan 1992, 269).

QUESTIONS OF ACCOUNTABILITY. Ensuring accountability, a fundamental feature of a sound tax system, is particularly difficult in the area of targeted tax incentives. One of the greatest problems is that tax incentive deals are often shrouded in secrecy. In many states, incentive deals are exempt from public disclosure laws; in some states, even the legislators are not privy to the details of tax incentive negotiations or agreements (Hancock 1999). Accountability is also problematic because states offering targeted incentives have little guarantee that the expected economic windfall will materialize or even that the business will carry out its expansion plans. State governments that are unwilling or unable to place meaningful restrictions on incentive recipients add to this problem. For example, only 9 states have reporting requirements for companies that receive incentives, and 25 states lack formal guidelines to determine whether a business adheres to the incentive requirements (LeRoy 1994).

Although accountability remains one of the most serious tax incentive issues, states have taken steps to alleviate some of the problem. To date, the most aggressive form of control has been the use of "clawbacks," statutory or contractual terms that force the recipient company to pay back all incentives if it fails to perform. Such laws have been passed in Vermont (Stat. Ann. tit. 10, sec. 264), Ohio (sec. 122.17), Connecticut (sec. 12-217[m]), and Nebraska (sec. 77-4101).

Another method for building accountability into targeted tax incentives is the use of quality job standards. In many states, companies receiving tax benefits must create jobs paying above-average wages and benefits. Largely because of efforts by advocacy groups such as Citizens for Tax Justice and Good Jobs First, the number of state and local jurisdictions requiring job quality standards increased from 6 in 1994 to 66 in 2000 (Duran 2000).

More stringent reporting requirements can also improve accountability. Illinois, for example, mandates that companies file reports before receiving incentives. West Virginia requires the governor to report on all incentive programs for which tax revenue has been allocated to evaluate costs and benefits. States can also utilize sunset provisions stipulating that unless the legislature renews the incentive law, a given tax incentive will automatically expire (Schweke, Rist, and Dabson 1994). The advantage of sunset provisions is that they force legislatures to evaluate the effectiveness of the incentives (presumably, with public input).

One of the most serious barriers to accountability is the states' failure to monitor and evaluate incentive programs. Although tax incentives abound, the states do not conduct regular or meaningful reviews of the programs to determine whether they are producing the anticipated economic outcomes. A recent study reached several troubling conclusions about the effectiveness of states' assessment efforts. First, performance auditing of development agencies is not frequent or thorough enough. Second, only 17 states require regular performance audits by the oversight agencies; of those states, 4 are regularly behind schedule on these audits. Third, in some states, audits of economic development are conducted only once every 15 years (Good Jobs First 2000).

TARGETED TAX INCENTIVES: A SOUND POLICY CHOICE? Should states employ targeted tax incentives in their efforts to compete for economic development? According to all available evidence, the answer is no. Research suggests that neither tax incentives nor state and local taxes significantly affect a company's location decisions (Due 1961). Additional studies have found that state tax policy matters little to businesses that want to move (Carlton 1983; Hekman 1982; Kieschnick 1981; Schmenner 1982). Moreover, nearly every econometric study of the subject concludes that state and local taxes do not necessarily attract business, create jobs, or enhance the economy (Lynch 1996; Wasylenko and McGuire 1985; Wilson 1989).

The lack of correlation between tax incentives and location decisions is understandable because state and local taxes are a very small part of the cost of doing business: One calculation puts them at less than 2 percent (Lynch 1996). Because the state tax burden is so low, after-tax rates of profit do not vary significantly from state to state. A more likely factor in swaying location decisions—and spurring economic growth—is investment in infrastructure (Bartik 1991). Many studies show that infrastructure investments—for example, in improving transportation systems (Wyaat 1994) and education (Helms 1985)—increase economic development.

A more fundamental reason for avoiding the use of targeted tax incentives is their inherent inequity. In the current system, a corporation need only hint at leaving a state, and political leaders invariably offer significant tax relief.

This environment has given rise to a number of examples where companies that have no real intention of leaving a state threaten to do so in order to receive the tax benefits. In 1999, Marriott International Corp. threatened to move its headquarters from suburban Maryland to Virginia, partly because Virginia had offered $6 million in tax incentives. Maryland, wishing to retain one of its premier employers, offered the hotel company nearly $44 million in property tax incentives. Marriott accepted Maryland's offer. It later turned out that during the negotiations, Marriott had decided to remain in Maryland—with or without the tax incentives (Brunori 1999).

In 1987, agricultural and food processing giant ConAgra, Inc., which was looking to expand its headquarters, threatened to leave Nebraska unless the state essentially overhauled its system for taxing business activity. In response to this threat, Nebraska lowered its income tax rate; exempted food processing equipment, corporate aircraft, and computers from its property tax; and refunded sales taxes paid for depreciable property (Schweke, Rist, and Dabson 1994). The state also granted tax incentives to ConAgra to expand its headquarters in Omaha. It turned out that ConAgra had never seriously considered leaving the state. Looking back, Senator Don Wesely of the Nebraska Unicameral Legislature called the ConAgra action "blackmail" (Wesely 1993, 646).

State legislators often have no way of determining whether a corporation is seriously considering a move, and are often pressured into granting relief. Even if the legislature could determine whether a corporation was seriously contemplating a move, few would argue that tax policy should be formed in this way.[7]

In many incentive deals, the states essentially surrender their policy-making obligations to the corporations seeking tax deals. From a policy-making perspective, one of the most detrimental facets of targeted tax incentives is that they compel businesses to negotiate tax burdens by playing one jurisdiction against another. As long as states are willing to bid for business, companies will demand incentive packages to relocate to, expand within, or remain in certain states.

State Tax Policy and Interstate Competition

Competition among the states is inevitable, especially as capital and labor become increasingly mobile. The political pressures to create jobs and to foster economic development further fuel competition.

As noted earlier, the states have essentially two choices when it comes to interstate competition. States can compete by providing high-quality public services and imposing tax burdens consistent with those imposed by other states. Alternatively, states can compete by offering targeted tax incentives to particular businesses to entice them to relocate to or remain in the state. From a good government and sound tax policy perspective, investing in services and maintaining competitive tax burdens is the better course of action. Forming policy through targeted tax incentives leads to inequities and inefficiencies. But how do legislators emphasize the positive aspects of competition while minimizing the use of targeted tax incentives?

No state will unilaterally forgo the use of incentives. The few cooperative agreements among the states to stop tax incentives did not work. For example, in 1991, Connecticut, New Jersey, New York, and New York City signed an agreement promising not to offer incentives to companies in the other tax jurisdictions. Within one year, New Jersey broke the agreement (by offering incentives to a New York firm), and within three years each of the signatories was routinely offering incentives to the others' companies (Barlett and Steele 1998).

Another option is federal legislation that would effectively end the use of targeted tax incentives. Congress has the power, under the Commerce Clause of the Constitution, to prohibit states from poaching business from other states. But federal controls over the state economic development authority are unlikely to garner the political support needed to solve the problems of targeted tax incentives. The states have traditionally opposed federal government encroachment on their taxing authority. That opposition, however, may soften in the face of serious problems posed by targeted tax competition.

Other, less drastic, initiatives could help curtail the use of targeted tax incentives. First, experts on fair and efficient tax policy need to educate legislators on the perils of targeted tax incentives. Most state legislators would oppose such policies if they understood all the facts. Few lawmakers would endorse tax incentives if they knew that such incentives were unnecessary and that they would result in a more complicated and less fair tax system.

Second, experts in the field of tax policy must better educate the public. The key to influencing lawmakers on the subject of tax incentives is making information on their use available to the public and press. Widespread public disclosure of incentive deals is necessary to understanding the severity and consequences of the problem. The public, press, and legislators could then evaluate the use of incentives. More public scrutiny would likely lead to fewer tax incentives.

Targeted tax incentives are pervasive, and it will likely take years of education to overcome the bias in favor of their use. If states continue to offer incentives, they should impose safeguards to protect the public's fiscal interests. States should adopt laws requiring that all benefits received by a particular company be repaid if that company fails to make the promised investments in capital and jobs. Moreover, states should require all corporations receiving tax incentives to abide by high-quality job standards. Under such arrangements, corporations must create jobs that provide pay and benefits well above the area's average pay and benefits so that the general population as well as large corporations benefit from the incentives.

Finally, states must conduct meaningful audits and evaluations of tax incentive programs to determine if they are producing a level of economic development that justifies continuing the incentive. Such audits should not only evaluate the corporate beneficiary's conduct (to ensure compliance with all terms) but also the effects of the incentive deal on the state's overall economy.

NOTES

1. As early as 1791, New Jersey offered tax abatements to induce Alexander Hamilton to locate his manufacturing plant in that state (Levine 1997).

2. Several legal scholars have recently challenged this traditional view. Enrich (1996) and Hellerstein and Coenen (1996) have argued that certain types of state tax incentives provided only to companies investing in the state may violate the Commerce Clause.

3. The old city political machines of Hague, Pendergast, and Daley were built on job creation. While the big cities were the most notorious for their patronage systems, many state governments ran well-oiled machines as well. Until the mid-20th century, virtually all state employees in Pennsylvania were political appointees of the governor. And in Virginia, during much of the past century, all state employees owed their jobs to the Byrd machine.

4. For a discussion of this proliferation in targeted tax incentives, see Brunori (1997).

5. In addition, many political leaders, business groups, and conservative organizations have criticized tax incentives. See Brunori (1997) and Barlett and Steele (1998).

6. For example, former Tennessee Governor Lamar Alexander (R) admitted that his state's incentive packages to Nissan and GM-Saturn, of $10 million and $17 million, respectively, were too large because those automakers were already likely to locate in Tennessee (Hamilton 1994). In another example, South Carolina probably would have secured a BMW plant even without offering incentives, given the state's high level of skilled labor (Waugh and Waugh 1991, 231). If companies are likely to make the desired investments in a state, the granting of unnecessary incentive packages will have a direct negative impact on that state's revenue.

7. While just a few examples are used to illustrate the problem, there are literally hundreds of cases in which companies threaten to relocate in order to receive tax benefits.

REFERENCES

Barlett, Donald L., and James B. Steele. 1998. "Corporate Welfare." *Time* (November 9).

Bartik, Timothy. 1991. "Who Benefits from State and Local Economic Development Policies?" Kalamazoo, Mich.: W.E. Upjohn Institute for Employment Research.

———. 1996. "Growing State Economies: How Tax and Public Services Affect Private Sector Performance." Washington, D.C.: Economic Policy Institute.

Brunori, David. 1997. "Principles of Tax Policy and Targeted Tax Incentives." *State and Local Government Review* 29 (1, winter): 50–61.

———. 1999. "Interview with Greg LeRoy on Incentives and Accountability." *State Tax Notes* (September 27): 837–839.

———. 2000a. "Everything I Know about Tax Incentives I Learned in New York." *State Tax Notes* (October 9): 963–964.

———. 2000b. "Is There a Silver Bullet for Targeted Tax Incentives?" *State Tax Notes* (January 10): 125–126.

Carlton, D. 1983. "The Location and Employment Choices of New Firms." *Review of Economics and Statistics* 65 (3): 440–449.

Due, John. 1961. "Studies of State-Local Tax Influences on Location of Industry." *National Tax Journal* 14: 50–60.

Duncan, Harley. 1988. "State Legislators and Tax Administrators: Can We Talk?" In *State Tax Reform: The Unfinished Agenda*, edited by Steven Gold. Denver, Colo.: National Conference of State Legislatures.

———. 1992. "Interstate Tax Competition: The Good, the Bad, and the Ugly." *State Tax Notes* (August 24): 266–270.

Duran, Rachel. 2000. "The End of the Candy Store? Many Communities Tie Job Quality Standards to Incentives." *Business Xpansion* (September).

Enrich, Peter D. "Saving the States from Themselves: Commerce Clause Constraints on State Tax Incentives for Business." *Harvard Law Review* 377 (December): 424–425.

Good Jobs First. 2000. "Minding the Candy Store: State Audits of Economic Development." Washington, D.C.: Institute on Taxation and Economic Policy.

Grady, Dennis. 1987. "State Economic Development Incentives: Why Do States Compete?" *State and Local Government Review* 19 (3, fall): 86–94.

Hamilton, Amy. 1994. "State Paid Too Much to Lure Mercedes-Benz, Former Tennessee Governor Says." *State Tax Notes* (November 7): 1316.

Hancock, Jay. 1999. "S.C. Pays Dearly for Added Jobs." *Baltimore Sun,* October 12.

Harrison, Bennett, and Sandra Kanter. 1978. "The Political Economy of States' Job Creation Business Incentives." *AIP Journal* 44 (October): 424.

Hekman, John. 1982. "Survey of Location Decisions in the South." *Economic Review* (June): 6–19.

Hellerstein, Walter, and Dan T. Coenen. 1996. "Commerce Clause Restraints of State Business Development Incentives." *Cornell Law Review* 81 (4): 789–878.

Helms, Jay. 1985. "The Effect of State and Local Taxes on Economic Growth: A Time Series Cross-Section Approach." *Review of Economics and Statistics* 67 (4): 574–582.

Kenyon, Daphne, and John Kincaid, eds. 1991. *Competition among States and Local Governments.* Washington, D.C.: Urban Institute Press.

Kieschnick, Michael. 1981. *State Taxation Policy.* Durham, N.C.: Duke University Press.

Kincaid, John. 1991. "The Competitive Challenge to Cooperative Federalism." In *Competition among States and Local Governments*, edited by Daphne Kenyon and John Kincaid. Washington, D.C.: Urban Institute Press.

LeRoy, Greg. 1994. "No More Candy Store." Washington, D.C.: Grassroots Policy Project.

Levine, Michael. 1997. "Can Tax Incentives Help Revitalize the Inner City?" *State Tax Notes* (September 15): 697–706.

Lynch, Robert. 1996. "Do State and Local Tax Incentives Work?" Washington, D.C.: Economic Policy Institute.

Musgrave, Richard. 1959. *The Theory of Public Finance.* New York: McGraw-Hill.

Noto, Nonna. 1991. "Trying to Understand the Economic Development Official's Dilemma." In *Competition among States and Local Governments,* edited by Daphne Kenyon and John Kincaid. Washington, D.C.: Urban Institute Press.

Oates, Wallace, E. 1972. *Fiscal Federalism.* New York: Harcourt, Brace, Jovanovich.

Pomp, Richard. 1998. "The Future of the State Income Tax: Reflections (and Confessions) of a Tax Lawyer." In *The Future of State Taxation,* edited by David Brunori (49–72). Washington, D.C.: Urban Institute Press.

Reschovsky, Andrew. 1998. "The Progressivity of State Tax Systems." In *The Future of State Taxation*, edited by David Brunori (161–190). Washington, D.C.: Urban Institute Press.

Schmenner, Roger W. 1982. *Making Business Location Decisions*. Englewood Cliffs, N.J.: Prentice Hall.

Schweke, William, Carl Rist, and Brian Dabson. 1994. *Bidding for Business*. Washington, D.C.: Corporation for Enterprise Development.

Shannon, John. 1991. "Federalism's Invisible Regulation—Interstate Competition." In *Competition among States and Local Governments,* edited by Daphne Kenyon and John Kincaid. Washington, D.C.: Urban Institute Press.

Spindler, Charles, and John Forrester. 1993. "Economic Development: Preferences among Models." *Urban Affairs Review* 29 (1): 28–53.

Vaughan, Roger. 1979. "State Taxation and Economic Development." Washington, D.C.: Council of State Planning Agencies.

Walker, Lee. 1989. "Economic Development in the States: The Changing Arena." Washington, D.C.: Council of State Governments.

Wasylenko, Michael, and Therese McGuire. 1985. "Jobs and Taxes: The Effect of Business Climate on States' Employment Growth Rates." *National Tax Journal* 38 (December): 497–511.

Waugh, William, and Deborah Waugh. 1991. "The Political Economy of Seduction: Promoting Business Relocation and Economic Development in Nonindustrial States." In *Public Policy and Economic Institutions,* edited by Melvin J. Dubnick and Alan Gitelson (221–234). Greenwich, Conn.: JAI Press.

Wesely, Don. 1993. "Myths and Realities of Economic Development Incentives: Who's Giving Away the Store? Revisited." *State Tax Notes* (September 20): 645–648.

Wilson, Roger. 1989. "State Business Incentives and Economic Growth: Are They Effective?" Lexington, Ky.: Council of State Governments.

Wolman, Harold. 1988. "Local Economic Development Policy: What Explains the Divergence between Policy Analysis and Political Behavior?" *Journal of Urban Affairs* 19 (1): 19–33.

Wyaat, Cathleen. 1994. "Zero Sum Games." *State Government News* (April): 28–32.

4

The Politics of State Taxation

*I can vote against a tax break for the elderly—
if I don't want to get reelected.*

—State legislator considering a tax measure
targeted to senior citizens

Taxes pay for an organized society. And the overwhelming majority of Americans would surely acknowledge that they receive something of value for their tax dollars. Still, like every public policy issue, taxes should be the subject of meaningful political debate, and citizens should have a voice in how their tax systems work. After all, taxes, by definition, are not voluntary. Few areas that involve government are more politically controversial than taxation, primarily because the underlying issues require normative value judgments that defy measurable parameters.

The questions behind taxation decisions are fundamental to forming sound policy. Who should pay for public services: The rich? The poor? The middle class? Individuals? Businesses? An equally pertinent question is who should be relieved from the burdens of taxation. Again, the questions are fundamental. Who should receive a break: Groups that provide economic growth and jobs? Charitable organizations? Veterans? Families? The disabled? The economically dispossessed? The possibilities are virtually endless. Strong, heartfelt arguments for tax relief are made every year on behalf of various segments of society.

The notion that tax laws should be constructed in a manner that benefits particular groups runs counter to the basic principles of sound tax policy. Rather, tax laws should minimize distinctions as to base and taxpayer (see chapter 2). Nonetheless, the states' tax laws are in fact shaped by political preferences. Virtually every legislative session and statewide election features proposals to provide tax relief to, or to impose a greater tax burden upon, a particular group.

In many instances, the call for tax relief rings from politically powerful constituencies. For example, most political leaders are cautious in opposing tax breaks for groups that have widespread public support, such as the elderly, children, families, and education. Many political leaders are also cautious in opposing tax breaks for businesses that are meant to spur job creation and thereby improve the economic environment of the state.

When money must be raised to pay for services demanded by the public, politics plays an equally important role in deciding who will shoulder a greater share of the burden. The politically influential groups that normally receive tax breaks are not likely to be targeted. However, because virtually all segments of society have their supporters and sympathizers, taxation can be politically perilous no matter who bears the greatest burden of paying for government. These competing interests often result in policy decisions that minimize taxes.

The Political Arenas

Traditionally, the politics of state taxation have been played out in two arenas: at the ballot box and in front of the legislature. Despite the lofty principles described in chapter 2, almost every tax policy argument is meant to influence either elections or the enactment of laws. The issues considered at the voting booth and in legislative sessions share some similarities. Electoral politics generally entail convincing a majority of voters (or, at least, a plurality of votes) to support a given candidate. Of course, a candidate often uses taxes to convince voters to support his or her party. Indeed, taxation has been a deciding factor in many state gubernatorial and legislative elections over the past quarter-century.

Legislative politics are more complex than electoral politics. Politicians use the legislative process to accomplish many goals. First, they must satisfy the needs and desires of constituents, particularly among their political supporters. Second, they must strive to make the state appear economically competitive relative to other states. A state that keeps tax burdens for businesses and individuals relatively low, especially for the politically influential, is often perceived as competitive. Third, legislators must find the money to pay for the public services demanded by their constituents. Roads, schools, police, and a host of other services require the states to raises billions of dollars in revenue every year. Like the political obstacles to raising taxes, which continue to increase, the need to raise revenue to provide services demanded by the public proceeds without respite. Both electoral and legislative tax politics essentially involve determining who will pay for government services and who will be granted tax relief.

While legislative and electoral politics remain the primary determinants of state tax policy, another political force is shaping our laws. State tax policy is increasingly formed through "direct democracy," a controversial process that allows citizens either to initiate or to approve changes to state laws. In the following sections, we discuss the effects of electoral politics, legislative politics, and direct democracy on taxation.

Electoral Politics and Tax Policy

Electoral politics shape tax policy in two important ways. First, politicians seeking office typically raise broad issues of state tax policies and commit to addressing those issues while in office. Candidates (and incumbents seeking reelection) usually focus on whether tax burdens are too high or, less frequently, too low. Electoral politics deal with easily understood tax concepts. For example, campaigns tout broad tax cuts or the elimination of unfair taxes. Sometimes candidates will advocate more targeted tax policies aimed at "hot-button" political issues such as tax relief for education and senior citizens or elimination of the sales tax on food.

As a general rule, candidates rarely propose or discuss narrow issues such as the creation or elimination of exemptions, deductions, or credits. They will also rarely, if ever, address subjects such as accelerated depreciation, sale for resale exemptions, formulary apportionment, or combined reporting. Even if candidates or their supporters have an interest in these technical aspects of tax policy, they will typically wait until they take office to address them.

In this regard, most candidates' approaches to tax policy are similar to their public approaches on most policy issues. Elections focus on broad-based issues such as quality of education, crime rates, and the need for improved transportation systems. Although candidates sometimes provide details of how they will accomplish particular policy goals, their campaigns generally stress "big-picture" issues. This broad approach contrasts sharply with legislative tax politics, which deals with the narrow issues of tax policy on a daily basis.

The second way electoral politics shape tax policy is by reinforcing the antitax culture that has taken root in the United States. Since the end of the Ford administration in the mid-1970s, American political discourse has been dominated by what can be called the "politics of antitaxation." Candidates in both parties, and at all levels of government, have more often than not campaigned against government in general and against taxes in particular.

This trend has prevailed not only at the state level but also at the executive level. Jimmy Carter made tax reform an important part of his platform. Ronald Reagan was elected in part on a promise to significantly cut federal taxes. In his 1988 campaign, George Bush made his ill-fated promise of "no new taxes." Republicans gained control of the U.S. Senate in 1982 and both houses of Congress in 1994 in part because of their antitax platform. Bill Clinton based his campaign to some extent on middle-class and low-income tax cuts. Most recently, George W. Bush made a pledge to cut more than $1 trillion in taxes the centerpiece of his campaign.

Recent history is also replete with examples of gubernatorial and legislative candidates pledging to cut—or at least to not raise—taxes. Moreover, few, if any, candidates have successfully campaigned on a promise to increase tax burdens. Even candidates who have run on platforms calling for expanded public services have been careful to avoid discussion about how those services would be financed. Where taxes have been a significant part of the campaign, the candidate advocating reducing tax burdens has prevailed more often than not.

Most of the well-known examples of electoral tax politics have occurred in gubernatorial campaigns.[1] Whether incumbents or challengers, candidates for the state executive office have used tax policy to advance their campaign prospects. Incumbent governors often advocate tax cuts in the years preceding an election (for a general discussion of such advocacy, see Howard [1994]). And an ample amount of evidence suggests that voters judge incumbent governors on their tax policies—in particular on whether their tax policies would increase tax burdens (Besley and Case 1995; Bowler and Donovan 1995; Kone and Winters 1993; Niemi, Stanley, and Vogel 1995). Consequently, both incumbents and challengers have heavily weighed the political risks of advocating or implementing tax increases (Berry and Berry 1992).[2]

In virtually every gubernatorial race, taxes are an issue to some extent (Brunori 2000). In some instances, taxes play only a peripheral part in the election, with candidates generally promising to reduce tax burdens. Tax policy tends to take a backseat when the incumbent administration has not significantly increased tax burdens or when the electorate is not concerned with issues of tax fairness. However, in many cases, tax policy is the most important (and sometimes the only) issue raised by candidates.

EXAMPLE ONE: FLORIO VERSUS WHITMAN. In 1993, New Jersey Governor Jim Florio (D) was seeking reelection. No incumbent governor in the state had been defeated in the 20th century. During his initial term, however, Florio faced a budget crisis largely inherited from his Republican predecessor. The budget crisis was exacerbated by the faltering economy and Florio's significant expansion of public services. The resulting fiscal problems forced Florio and the Democratically controlled legislature to raise both income and sales taxes in 1990 by an unprecedented $2.8 billion.

Florio's challenger in the election was Christine Todd Whitman. Whitman was a relatively unknown Republican Party activist when she came within a thousand votes of beating Democrat Bill Bradley in the U.S. Senate race in 1990. Whitman, a moderate by modern GOP standards, used her strong showing in that race as the basis for a challenge to Florio. In a well-orchestrated campaign, Whitman hammered Florio on the sharp tax increases that occurred in his administration. Virtually every aspect of Whitman's campaign focused on the tax increases during Florio's tenure as governor.

Whitman did more than criticize Florio. She promised to drastically cut the state's income tax rate by 30 percent over three years. Florio, sensing the popular dissatisfaction with the tax increases, also promised significant tax cuts. By that time, however, the Whitman campaign had successfully connected high taxes with the Florio administration.

In the end, Whitman won a crushing victory against Florio. Just how successful Whitman was in creating the impression that Florio was "pro-tax" is evident from later campaigns. In 2000, Florio campaigned for the Democratic nomination for the U.S. Senate. His opponent, Wall Street executive and political unknown Jon Corzine, used the same arguments regarding taxes to prevent Florio's comeback.

EXAMPLE TWO: GILMORE VERSUS BEYER. Another example of electoral tax politics occurred in Virginia during the 1997 gubernatorial campaign. The race pitted State Attorney General Jim Gilmore (R) against popular Lieutenant Governor Don Beyer (D). During the campaign, Gilmore seized upon an issue that had been festering in the commonwealth for years: the property tax on motor vehicles.

The property tax on motor vehicles was arguably the most unpopular of Virginia's taxes. Owners of automobiles registered in the state had to pay a tax on the market value of the cars. The revenue from the tax was split between the local governments administering the tax and the state. Car owners had to pay the tax in a single payment in the late fall, which meant that owners of new vehicles were greeted with large tax bills (totaling hundreds, often thousands, of dollars) just before the holidays. The automobile dealers in the state also disliked the tax because they believed it deterred new car purchases.

In a brilliant political move, Gilmore pledged early in his 1997 campaign to end the car tax, a promise that resonated with voters throughout the state. Because much of the car tax revenue went to local governments, city and county political leaders were expected to oppose its elimination. By pledging to use state funds to replace the lost local revenue, Gilmore prevented serious opposition from local interests.

The Gilmore camp quickly turned the car tax into the flagship issue of the campaign. The rhetoric behind the campaign illustrated the prominence of this one issue. "No Car Tax" bumper stickers were soon spotted all over the state. Gilmore made ending the car tax the focal point of virtually every speech.

When Gilmore first made his promise to end the car tax, the Beyer campaign roundly criticized the proposal. The Beyer camp said that the state could not afford to pay for abolishing the tax. It also pointed out that replacing the local car tax revenue with state-appropriated funds did not guarantee that local governments would have the resources to fund services. Finally, the Beyer campaigned warned that local government leaders from both parties would lose autonomy because the state funds would inevitably come with strings attached.

The Gilmore campaign disputed the charges lodged by Beyer, but the technical aspects of the proposal were largely immaterial. Voters in

Virginia overwhelmingly supported repeal of the dreaded car tax. Sensing the overwhelming support for repeal, the Beyer campaign proposed its own plan to end the car tax. But the issue was clearly Gilmore's. Gilmore's car-tax campaign culminated in an overwhelming victory over Don Beyer. Although Virginia had steadily been moving into the Republican camp, Gilmore's victory over the popular Democrat was due in large part to the car-tax issue.

Legislative Politics and State Tax Policy

Legislative tax politics—the process by which tax changes are proposed, enacted, and signed into law—involve both the executive and legislative branches. In many respects, legislative tax politics are a gubernatorial phenomenon, because in most states the governor first proposes the budget. For the purposes of our discussion, "legislative" describes the overall process and not just the work of state representatives and senators.

Legislative tax politics differ significantly from electoral tax politics in their focus. While electoral tax politics are aimed at broad segments of the voting public, legislative tax politics usually involve a more limited number of individuals. Legislation on tax policies does affect the general population. Indeed, such decisions, mostly in the form of rate changes, occur on a yearly basis. But significant reforms occur infrequently. Rather, the routine work of the legislature involves proposing and adopting incremental changes to the tax laws. Most of these changes usually benefit, or otherwise affect, a small segment of society. These groups can be expected to try to influence state legislators on policy outcomes.

In this regard, taxation is no different from any other public policy issue. Interest groups try to influence legislators to obtain favorable tax treatment. Not surprisingly, the most effective and well-financed lobbying efforts are usually conducted by the business community. Studies have found that business organizations have more influence when they appear before the legislative branch than any other interest group (Bingham, Hawkins, and Hebert 1978; Thomas and Hrebenar 1999).

Of course, not all lobbyists are working for large corporations. Small business interests, labor unions, local government associations, and civic associations all influence state tax issues. Even environmental groups attempt to influence state legislators on particular tax issues.[3]

MOTIVATIONS FOR LEGISLATORS. State legislators formulate tax policy to further a number of public policy and political goals. These goals often intersect when a particular tax policy can enhance a legislator's standing with an important special interest group.

State legislators are concerned with getting reelected, furthering their careers, and enhancing their political reach. Legislators' actions, whether they benefit political benefactors or are in the public interest, are often guided by ambition. Thus, state lawmakers are acutely aware of the political ramifications of their votes and positions on tax issues. Those groups that are crucial to a legislator's political career can usually count on the legislator to support tax policies that benefit their interests. For example, lawmakers who rely heavily on the business community for financial support will tend to vote to minimize business tax burdens. Similarly, lawmakers counting on relatively wealthy suburban voters may support reductions in personal income taxes or the granting of education tax benefits. And legislators from inner-city districts may look for ways to ease regressivity.

Political motivations give rise to extensive lobbying efforts among those groups affected by state tax policy. Individuals, businesses, and other organizations with a stake in the policy debate continually pressure legislators. And legislators, faced with future campaign needs, often heed their concerns.

PAY FOR PUBLIC SERVICES. Legislators must raise sufficient revenue to pay for the public services demanded by their constituents. Because most states have strict balanced budget requirements, legislators must be willing to impose tax burdens on people and businesses that approximately equal the costs of providing those government services— regardless of antitaxation sentiment and concerns about interstate competition. Legislative tax politics generally involve determining who will pay for those services.

The kinds of services that the government chooses to fund is outside the scope of this discussion; however, it's worth noting that some hot-button issues (in particular, education and public safety) are sure to prompt legislatures to find additional revenue even at the risk of raising taxes. As noted in chapter 2, state legislators have shown a strong ability to raise the revenue necessary to fund public services. The political pressure to fund public services should not be understated. Governors and legislators alike are judged by their constituents on the quality and quantity of public services provided.

HIDE THE TAX (OR EXPORT IT). Political leaders at all levels of government seek to obscure tax burdens by levying taxes that are largely unnoticed by the citizens (Dye 1990; Hansen 1983; Steuerle 1991). One recent study found that state representatives would almost always attempt to obscure taxes (Beamer 1999). By hiding tax burdens, political leaders can create the illusion of paying for public services without the attendant tax burdens. Excise taxes and corporate income taxes can sometimes be hidden. Those burdens are often passed onto consumers, who may not realize that the embedded additional cost is the result of government action. The sales tax, however, provides the best example of an easily hidden tax because it is paid in small increments by citizens who are largely unaware of their overall sales-tax burden.

The desire to obscure tax burdens adds to the regressivity of state tax systems. Often, state lawmakers concentrate on reducing income taxes, one of our most progressive but highly visible taxes. At the same time, lawmakers seek to retain the less visible, but more regressive, consumption taxes. As one scholar notes, "Taxes with low visibility are simply less politically advantageous to decrease" (Beamer 1999, 37).

Another bias exhibited by state lawmakers is, whenever possible, to export the tax burden out of state to individuals and firms. Some types of taxes are particularly well suited for exportation. One example is severance taxes on natural resources that will be consumed out of state. In states with significant tourist industries (e.g., Florida, Nevada), much of the consumption taxes (general sales and excise) will be exported to people who live outside the state. And corporate income tax apportionment formulas can be constructed so that companies operating primarily out of state pay most corporate income tax revenue.[4]

FUEL ECONOMIC DEVELOPMENT. State legislatures generally seek policies that appear to foster economic development. Accordingly, legislators from both parties favor tax policies that are perceived to encourage economic development and job creation. Because economic development benefits virtually all segments of society, endorsing tax policies that appear to promote economic growth fits into most legislators' political agendas. For example, tax incentives for corporations can be used to satisfy both business interests (by reducing the taxes on capital and profits) and individuals (by promising more and better jobs).

In every state, during every legislative session, lawmakers are confronted with numerous proposals that purportedly will make the state more attractive to business.[5] Because of their interest in creating jobs and spurring economic development, state legislators are inclined to opt for tax policies favored by the business community. Policymakers' sensitivity to the needs of business has made government accommodation of business demands routine and familiar (Lindblom 1997).

BIAS TOWARD REGRESSIVITY. Another important aspect of legislative tax politics, and one closely related to the desire to spur economic development, is lawmakers' apparent bias toward regressivity. State legislators have shown a tendency to favor reducing progressive taxes, such as personal and corporate income taxes, and raising more regressive taxes, such as consumption taxes.

A recent study by the National Conference of State Legislators found that 34 states reduced net taxes by an aggregate $7.3 billion in the 1999 legislative sessions (NCSL 2000). In those cuts, the states were far more likely to forgo progressive personal income taxes than any other levy. Twenty-eight states reduced their personal income tax burdens by $2.7 billion in 1999, for the fifth straight year of significant cuts in their income taxes. Only three states—Arizona, Montana, and Wisconsin—raised net income taxes that year, and even those states' relatively modest increases were due to the restructuring of their tax codes.

According to the NCSL study, states were also quick to cut corporate income and business taxes in 1999. A total of 17 states cut corporate income and business taxes, for a net reduction of nearly $1 billion. The business tax cuts in 1999 were about double those of the previous year. Only New Hampshire and Alabama enacted net business tax increases.

The study did find that 23 states reduced sales and use taxes by $3.2 billion. These numbers, however, are misleading. More than $2.6 billion of these cuts were in the form of onetime rebates offered in four states and thus did not represent permanent reductions in sales and use tax rates. Furthermore, about $99 million of the cuts were from sales-tax holidays enacted in Texas, New York, and Florida. Discounting for the rebates and tax holidays, the 1999 sales tax reductions were closer to the $659 million in cuts that occurred in 1998.

The bias in favor of keeping income and business taxes in check also occurs when times are tough and states face budget shortfalls. The Center on Budget and Policy Priorities (CBPP) conducted a study of state fiscal policy during the early 1990s, when the economy and state budgets were in decidedly worse condition than they are today. The CBPP study found that states needing additional revenue turned to the sales tax more quickly and often than the personal income tax (Johnson and Lav 1997).

There are several possible explanations for the regressive bias. Personal income taxes are more progressive than consumption taxes (sales, use, or excise). Thus, the wealthier a citizen becomes, the more he or she will gain (or lose) from cuts (or increases) in the income tax. This fact is well known to state political leaders. Moreover, political science research shows that the wealthier an individual is, the more likely he or she is to vote and to contribute to political campaigns. Thus, legislators view not increasing or even cutting personal income taxes as simply a matter of good politics.[6]

The same logic can be applied to business taxes, which every year account for a smaller percentage of state tax revenue. The business community is the most politically powerful special interest group in most states. Its economic clout has much to do with its favorable tax treatment.

The second possible reason for the bias in favor of regressivity is that state legislators believe that reducing income tax burdens will foster economic growth. As discussed in more detail in chapter 6, raising income taxes has always been viewed by political leaders as detrimental to economic development. Consumption taxes in general have rarely suffered from such suspicions. Although ample evidence refutes the argument that progressive income taxes necessarily deter growth (for example, see Reschovsky [1998]), that belief continues to be held by many state lawmakers.

The third possible explanation for the regressive bias is that legislators do not realize the implications of tax policy choices. Few states conduct incidence studies explaining which income groups will bear the burden of proposed tax changes (CBPP 1997). Legislators have little specific knowledge of the relative burdens placed on the poor, middle class, and wealthy by a change in tax law. To be sure, legislators generally recognize that income taxes are progressive and that consumption taxes are regressive. Given the politics of who pays and who votes, this limited knowledge might be enough to guide decisionmaking. Legislators, however, might make different choices if they understood the degree of variation in tax burdens across economic classes.

HELPING THE DISPOSSESSED. State legislators and governors routinely express concern for the poor and less-fortunate members of society. Tax policies purportedly aimed at alleviating tax burdens on the poor are proposed in virtually every legislative session by lawmakers from across the political spectrum. Many of these proposals are sincere attempts to assist low- and moderate-income taxpayers. Some of the proposals merely give the appearance of helping the less fortunate. Few of these proposals, however, actually reduce the regressivity of the system.

Even policies that ease sales taxes do not necessarily address regressivity. Although political leaders have succeeded in exempting many necessities from the sales tax, the wealthy and middle class enjoy the benefits of such exemptions to the same extent as, if not more than, the poor. Exempting food meant for home consumption also does not necessarily help the poorest segments of society. These individuals likely receive federal food-stamp assistance, which is already exempt from sales tax. Moreover, removing taxes from necessities results in greater tax rates for nonexempt items (Mikesell 1992).[7]

Legislators routinely advocate measures that to some extent reduce the tax burdens on low-income individuals. Many lawmakers recognize the unfairness of burdening those least able to pay the costs of government. The poor and dispossessed are also politically sympathetic. Unfortunately, much concern for the poor amounts to little more than lip service on the part of political leaders.

Direct Democracy and Tax Policy

Direct democracy, discussed as early as the Constitutional Convention in 1787, has been available in some states for more than a century. Its use in the tax policy arena, however, is a relatively new development. California's Proposition 13, enacted in 1978, jump-started the modern direct-democracy movement. Direct democracy allows citizens to adopt laws or to amend the state constitution independent of the legislature. In 16 states, citizens are allowed to put statutory or constitutional measures directly on the ballot for approval or rejection by the voters. In seven additional states, citizens must first submit statutory or constitutional changes to the legislature; if the legislature fails to approve the statute or constitutional amendment, the proponents may then submit the proposal directly to the voters.

Direct democracy has become an important component of American politics (Berry and Berry 1992; Brunori 1999b). Although a detailed discussion of the relationship between tax policy and direct democracy is outside the scope of this work, we examine several aspects of direct democracy essential to understanding tax politics.

THE PROLIFERATION OF INITIATIVES. Every year, hundreds of measures are put to popular vote in the 24 states that allow initiatives and popular referendums. The issues have included a wide range of public policy matters, such as animal rights, abortion, the death penalty, prayer in school, various business regulatory matters, environmental protection, and smoking. Taxes, however, are the issue most often placed on the ballots for voter approval. Between 1978 and 1999, citizens placed 130 tax initiatives on statewide ballots. During the 1990s, 170 tax measures have been put to a vote in initiative and referendum states.[8]

INITIATIVES, REFERENDUMS, AND TAX POLICY. Most initiatives and referendum in the tax area seek to limit states' power to tax. Of the 130 tax initiatives placed on the ballot since 1978, 86 would have restricted state taxing authority by setting limits on revenue or rates or by creating procedures that make raising revenue through taxation more difficult. Twenty-seven measures would have expanded state taxing authority by raising rates or adopting new types of taxes. Seventeen initiatives would have had a neutral effect on state taxing authority.

More significantly, limitations on state taxing authority were more likely to be approved by the voters than other types of initiatives. Of the 86 measures that would have placed limitations on taxation, 41 were successful, a passage rate of 48 percent. This passage rate is greater than that enjoyed by initiatives in general. Since 1978, only 41 percent of all initiatives submitted to the voters were passed. By contrast, only 10 (37 percent) of the 27 measures that would have *expanded* taxing power were passed. This imbalance is consistent with the decidedly antitax sentiment evident in the United States.

Given the political climate of the last quarter-century, the use of the initiative and referendum process to limit government tax powers is not surprising. Indeed, states that allow initiatives and referendums have had more restrictive tax limitations than states that do not allow initiatives and referendums (Matsusaka 1998). Initiatives and referendums, however, do not necessarily lead to smaller government and tax limitations.

During the early part of the 20th century, initiative and referendum states actually had greater tax and expenditure growth than states without the initiative and referendum process (Matsusaka 1998).

SETTING TAX POLICY THROUGH DIRECT DEMOCRACY. Direct democracy has become an increasingly controversial subject in American politics (see Broder [2000] and Schrag [1999]). Many policy issues arise in the context of direct democracy, especially as it pertains to tax policy. Moreover, much of the discussion has focused on direct democracy's negative implications for tax policy.

One oft-mentioned problem is that direct democracy has become dominated by wealthy special interest groups that use the process to bypass state legislators (Smith 1998). Legislators, of course, are criticized for being beholden to special interests. Direct democracy may also be coming under the same cloud.

Another argument against using direct democracy to determine taxation is that the public does not have the knowledge or expertise to evaluate sound tax policy. Debates over tax policy at federal and state levels have long been dominated by groups with significant training, education, and experience in public finance. Lobbyists and legislative staffs comprise tax lawyers, economists, and accountants who can evaluate the legal, budgetary, and economic consequences of tax policy choices. The need for specialization has become increasingly obvious as our state tax systems have become more sophisticated.

Direct democracy, however, places many of those decisions in the hands of a well-meaning but untrained voting public. The potential problems in relying on untrained voters are numerous. The public rarely knows the ramifications of significant tax cuts (e.g., services will have to be reduced or other taxes increased). Furthermore, the public typically does not know a proposal's consequences for economic development or interstate competition. They also have no way of gauging future spending and revenue needs.

More philosophically, direct democracy weakens representative government, the foundation of both our federal and state governments. The direct democracy movement bypasses the elected legislatures charged for the past 225 years with making laws. Despite some of the politics involved in lawmaking, the legislative system has served the American people well for more than two centuries.

The greatest limitation of direct democracy, however, is that it requires an up or down vote on tax policy measures. Voters must decide to approve or to reject a proposal. There is no room for compromise and no mechanism for negotiation. Thus, proponents of an initiative may recommend a $1 billion income-tax cut. The voters can accept or reject the reduction. But suppose the state can afford only a $750 million reduction? Or suppose reducing consumption or property taxes, rather than income taxes, would be wiser? Those types of questions can only be answered by the legislature.

Despite the problems associated with formulating tax policy through direct democracy, the process will continue to be used by conservative—and, increasingly, by liberal—groups (Brunori 1999b).

NOTES

1. The tax politics of legislative elections have not been studied by researchers or covered by the national press to the same extent as those for gubernatorial elections.

2. Of course, not all incumbents who support tax increases are defeated at reelection. Indeed, numerous incumbents who supported significant tax increases have won reelection (Winters 1999).

3. The perception that business opposes tax increases while labor organizations and public officials favor tax increases has also been found to be true (Bingham, Hawkins, and Hebert 1978).

4. In-state residents who do not bear the true costs have less connection to their government. They are not being asked to contribute to, and thus are less likely to participate in, public affairs. States operating this way run the risk of becoming unaccountable and inefficient; however, these concerns are more than overshadowed by the political advantages of exporting tax burdens.

5. A review of five years of proposed state tax legislation, made available by *State Tax Today*, reveals that an overwhelming majority of proposals (65 percent) were touted by their sponsors as promoting economic development.

6. The alternative—cutting regressive consumption taxes—has the opposite political effect. The poor have more to gain from sales tax cuts and more to lose from sales tax increases. But among the poor, voter turnout is smaller than among the wealthy.

7. Sales-tax holidays are another example of tax policies purportedly designed to assist the poorer segments of society. Several states exempt clothing during specified periods to afford low-income families the opportunity to shop tax free. Such holidays, however, rarely result in savings for shoppers (see Brunori [1999c]).

8. A collection of data on the use of initiatives and referendums to formulate tax policy—based on information from *State Tax Today* and the Initiative and Referendum Institute (http://www.iandrinstitute.org)—is available from the author.

REFERENCES

Beamer, Glenn. 1999. *Creative Politics: Taxes and Public Goods in a Federal System.* Ann Arbor, Mich.: University of Michigan Press.

Berry, Francis Stokes, and William D. Berry. 1992. "Tax Innovation in the States: Capitalizing on Political Opportunity." *American Journal of Political Science* 36 (3): 715–742.

Besley, Timothy, and Ann Case. 1995. "Incumbent Behavior: Vote-Seeking, Tax-Setting, and Yardstick Competition." *American Economic Review* 85 (1, March): 25–45.

Bingham, Richard D., Brett W. Hawkins, and F. Ted Hebert. 1978. *The Politics of State and Local Revenue.* New York: Praeger.

Bowler, Shaun, and Todd Donovan. 1995. "Popular Responsiveness to Taxation." *Political Research Quarterly* 48 (1): 79–99.

Broder, David. 2000. *Democracy Derailed: Initiative Campaigns and the Power of Money.* New York: Harcourt Brace.

Brunori, David. 1999a. "The Curious Case of Supermajorities." *State Tax Notes* (February 1): 325–326.

———. 1999b. "'The Politics of Taxation': Initiatives, Referendums Are Here to Stay." *State Tax Notes* (May 17): 1635–1637.

———. 1999c. "Sales Tax Holidays: Real Relief or Political Gimmicks?" *State Tax Notes* (December 6): 1521–1522.

———. 2000. "An Early Look at the Governors' Races." *State Tax Notes* (May 15): 1693–1695.

Dye, Thomas. 1990. *American Federalism: Competition among Governments.* Lexington, Mass.: Lexington Books.

Hansen, Susan B. 1983. *The Politics of Taxation: Revenue without Representation.* New York: Praeger.

Howard, Marcia. 1994. "A History Lesson." *State Tax Notes* (March 28): 831–820.

Johnson, Nicholas, and Iris Lav. 1997. "Are State Taxes Becoming More Regressive?" *State Tax Notes* (October 6): 893–895.

Kone, Susan L., and Richard Winters. 1993. "Taxes and Voting: Electoral Retribution in the American States." *Journal of Politics* 55 (1, February): 22–40.

Lindblom, Charles. 1977. *Politics and Markets.* New York: Basic Books.

Matsusaka, John. 1998. "Fiscal Effects of the Voter Initiative in the First Half of the Twentieth Century." *Journal of Law and Economics* 43 (2): 619–650.

Mikesell, John. 1992. "State Tax Policy in a Changing Economy." *Public Budgeting and Finance* (spring): 75–101.

National Conference of State Legislatures. 2000. *State Budget and Tax Actions 2000.* Washington, D.C.: author.

NCSL. *See* National Conference of State Legislatures.

Niemi, Richard G., Harold Stanley, and Ronald Vogel. 1995. "State Economies and State Taxes: Do Voters Hold Governors Accountable?" *American Journal of Political Science* 39: 936–957.

Reschovsky, Andrew. 1998. "The Progressivity of State Tax Systems." In *The Future of State Taxation,* edited by David Brunori (161–190). Washington, D.C.: Urban Institute Press.

Schrag, Peter. 1999. *Paradise Lost: California's Experience, America's Future*. Berkeley: University of California Press.

Smith, Daniel. 1998. *Tax Crusaders and the Politics of Direct Democracy*. New York: Routledge.

Steuerle, C. Eugene. 1991. *The Tax Decade: How Taxes Came to Dominate the Public Agenda*. Washington, D.C.: Urban Institute Press.

Thomas, Clive S., and Ronald J. Hrebenar. 1999. "Interest Groups in the States." In *Politics in the American States*, edited by Virginia Gray, Russell Hanson, and Herbert Jacob (113–143). Washington, D.C.: Congressional Quarterly Press.

Winters, Richard F. 1999. "The Politics of Taxing and Spending. In *Politics in the American States*, edited by Virginia Gray, Russell Hanson, and Herbert Jacob (304–348). Washington, D.C.: Congressional Quarterly Press.

5

Sales and Use Taxes

The sales tax cannot maintain its role within
the existing tax system.

—William Fox (1997)

Sales and use taxes are one of the most important sources of state revenue. For most of the past 50 years, the sales tax has raised more money than any other source, consistently accounting for more than a third of state tax revenue. In 1998, states raised over $156 billion from the sales tax (U.S. Census Bureau 2000).[1]

Forty-five states currently impose sales and use taxes. In 10 of those states, the sales tax accounts for more than 40 percent of tax revenue, with the state of Washington relying on the tax for nearly 60 percent of its tax revenue (Federation of Tax Administrators 1999).[2] Alaska, Delaware, Montana, New Hampshire, and Oregon do not impose state sales taxes, although Alaska allows local-option sales taxes. The states that do not impose a sales tax make up less than 3 percent of the U.S. population, which means that the overwhelming majority of Americans routinely pay these taxes.

In addition to raising a substantial portion of the revenue collected by the states and affecting the vast majority of the population, the sales tax is an integral part of a sophisticated system of intergovernmental public finance. Traditionally, the states have relied most heavily on consumption taxes, while the federal government has relied predominantly on income taxes. Local governments have counted on real property taxes to fund public services. Because the other levels of government have not used general consumption taxes to a great extent, the states have enjoyed much discretion in deciding how they levy sales taxes. This, in turn, has provided the states great flexibility in structuring their overall financial systems.

The sales and use tax faces many formidable challenges to its predominant role in state public finance. Constitutional, technological, economic, and political factors have all curbed the states' reliance on the tax. Despite the tax's durability over the past 50 years, it is questionable whether the sales and use tax will remain the dominant source of state government revenue finance. As a percentage of total state tax revenue, the sales tax has continued to fall since the 1970s. In 1998—for the first time—the personal income tax surpassed the sales tax as the leading source of revenue for the states. In 1998, the personal income tax accounted for almost 34 percent of state tax revenue, while the sales tax accounted for just under 33 percent. Public finance experts generally believe that personal income tax revenue will continue to grow as a percentage of state tax revenue, while sales tax revenue will continue to decline (Brunori 1999a).

Success of the Tax

Despite no longer being the single most dominant source of revenue, the sales tax has been one of the most reliable and stable sources of revenue for state governments for several reasons, including its established presence, its relatively low rates, and other positive features.

Wide Public Acceptance

The time-worn shibboleth that "an old tax is a good tax" helps explain the endurance of the sales tax. The tax, first implemented during the Great Depression, is ingrained in the American psyche and thus is widely accepted. Most Americans have lived their entire lives expecting to pay tax on their retail purchases of tangible personal property and express little surprise or anger when the cost of an item turns out to be higher than the stated price. Because of its established place in our lives, the sales tax complies with two notions thought to be necessary for a sound tax system: stability and predictability.

More cynically, some critics argue that the sales tax is politically acceptable because the people who are most adversely affected, poorer individuals, are least likely to voice their opposition on Election Day. Although the poor are less likely to vote or otherwise influence public finance choices, most scholars dismiss the notion that policymakers intentionally rely on consumption taxes for this reason. As noted tax scholar John Mikesell states:

> Some might argue that higher-income American political elites work to keep this regressive system, but I think ignorance and [lack of] interest are more likely explanations than systematic malice or manipulation. Substantial revenue, simple and convenient payment, and relatively low rates win out over regressivity in the political process (Brunori 1999a, 1367).

The public's acceptance of the sales tax is documented in opinion studies on society's view of the tax system. Although those surveyed admit they do not like taxes very much, they identify levies on consumption as among the most acceptable forms of taxation (Advisory Commission on Intergovernmental Relations 1993; Cole and Kincaid 2000).

Low Rates/Many Exemptions

The relatively small burden that consumers face in paying sales tax facilitates consumer acceptance of the tax. States impose sales and use taxes at rates ranging from 3 to 7 percent, and 30 states impose rates of less than 6 percent (Federation of Tax Administrators 1999). Although the tax may be significant on higher-priced goods, most people barely notice the small amounts on routine purchases. In addition, the annual tax burden is less noticeable than income tax to consumers because it is spread out over many purchases.

The states keep sales tax rates relatively low to minimize both the potential for tax evasion and the effects of interstate competition. States generally do not want to risk giving vendors incentive to sell goods without collecting sales and use tax. They also know that consumers, when it is practical, will shop in states with lower sales-tax burdens or will use remote venues that are generally exempt from the sales tax, such as mail-order centers or the Internet.

The exemption of many goods and services from the retail sales tax may boost consumer acceptance of the tax overall. For example, sales of services and intangible property are exempt in most states. These exclusions alone render more than half the economy exempt from sales tax. To curtail the inherent regressivity of the tax, most states also exempt items deemed as necessities. Food, prescription drugs, education, and, in some cases, clothing are largely exempt in most states. While policymakers and researchers debate whether such exemptions actually ease regressivity or otherwise promote fairness, most agree that the exemptions make the sales tax less noticeable and less burdensome for the average consumer. And the exemptions for necessities increase the public's acceptance immeasurably.

Ease of Administration and Compliance

Another reason for the long-running success of the sales tax is the ease and efficiency of both compliance and administration. The vendor collects the tax and remits payment to the state. In virtually all states, consumers pay the tax at the time of purchase. At that point, the taxpayer's responsibility with respect to the sales tax ends. The individual taxpayer has no forms to file, no records to keep, no accountants to pay, and no other costs generally associated with tax compliance. Since the federal government ended the deduction for sales tax payments as part of the 1986 Tax Reform Act, individual's do not need to keep records of purchases for tax purposes.

Businesses paying sales tax do incur some compliance costs because they must keep substantial records of their purchases and payments. Most businesses, however, already retain such records for federal tax purposes. Publicly traded corporations must also keep these records to comply with securities law. Thus, the added costs are not all that high.

Compliance with the sales tax law is more costly for vendors than for consumers. The vendor must determine the amount of the tax owed, collect the tax, keep records of the transactions, file returns, and make payments to the state. This process is even more complicated and expensive in states that offer many types of exemptions because it is up to the vendor to identify which of its products and services are taxable and which are exempt.

These compliance costs, however, are somewhat offset by laws allowing the vendor to retain part of the tax to defray the administrative expenses of collecting and remitting the tax. As of January 1, 1999, 30 of the 45 states imposing the tax provided some compensation to the vendor (Federation of Tax Administrators 1999).

For the state, the tax is relatively easy and efficient to administer. The vendor collects the tax and remits the payment to the state. If the vendor fails to collect the tax or make payment, it becomes liable for the amount of the tax and could face civil and criminal penalties. Because any market advantage in evading or avoiding the tax is more than offset by the possible penalties, most vendors comply with the law. Vendor compliance is especially likely among large and publicly traded companies.

Small businesses tend to incur greater costs in collecting and administering the sales tax than do larger businesses. Smaller businesses generally have fewer accounting controls and records of sales and are less likely to know the legal requirements of collecting tax from their customers. They are also more likely to have the ability and the motivation to avoid collection and remittance of tax. For these reasons, most of the state costs and efforts for administering the sales tax concentrate on small businesses.[3]

The ease of administration and compliance generally does not extend to vendors with many multistate transactions or to the use tax. Vendors with multistate transactions will likely experience numerous problems identifying what is and is not subject to tax in the 45 states and more than 6,000 localities that tax sales. Thus, businesses will incur added costs in complying with the tax laws in numerous jurisdictions. To some extent, technology designed to track tax-compliance requirements around the country has minimized these costs.

The use tax also can be difficult to collect. Because the tax is not typically collected by vendors selling remotely into a taxing state, remittance to the state is the responsibility of the consumer. Use tax compliance for individual consumers is abysmally low.[4] Consumers are largely unaware of, or choose to ignore, their legal responsibilities regarding the use tax. Even those individuals who are aware of the tax often neglect to keep records of their purchases. Others simply evade the tax. This noncompliance results in added difficulties for the states. Low levels of self-assessment force states to forgo much revenue unless they step up audits of individuals—an option that most revenue departments have found politically impossible.

To overcome some of the problems with use-tax compliance among individuals, some states have formed information-sharing agreements.

Under these agreements, state revenue departments are notified when residents receive shipments of taxable goods (usually with some minimum dollar value) from out of state. The revenue department then notifies the resident that use tax is due.

Other Virtues of the Sales Tax

The practical advantages of the sales tax include public acceptance and efficient administration. But there are more theoretical reasons for the success of the tax as well. Although these virtues may not be apparent to most taxpayers or even to government officials, they explain why the sales tax has been the dominant source of revenue for much of the past century.

First, while all taxes affect economic activity in some way, the sales tax is perceived to have less influence on business decisions than the state income tax. More important, the political perception is that income taxes, individual or corporate, deter economic development. As discussed in the next chapter, this perception has led to a bias in favor of consumption taxes over income taxes. The sales tax has never suffered such suspicion. Moreover, evidence shows that the sales tax has virtually no effect on the timing of business decisions; businesses and individuals generally do not delay or hasten decisions because of the tax (Mikesell 1998). Thus, relative to other levies, the sales tax complies, or at least complies more fully, with one of the most basic principles of sound tax policy: neutrality.

The sales tax has another advantage: It falls under a benefits-received theory of taxation that is generally accepted by the public. The sales tax assigns costs according to the spending of the individual. The level of consumption is a barometer for measuring the benefits received by the consumer (Mikesell 1998). Theoretically, the individual can vary the tax burden by adjusting his or her spending on taxable purchases, particularly if necessities (food, medicine, clothing, etc.) are excluded from the tax base. Moreover, assigning the costs of government according to consumption is consistent with the age-old American traditions of consumer sovereignty and private markets (Mikesell 1998).

Finally, sales tax is transparent; both liability and burden of payment are usually very clear. This is certainly true of the sales tax when it is levied on purchases by the final consumer. The transparency is largely the result of state laws forbidding vendors from disguising the tax. In most states, the sales tax must be itemized separately from the purchase price, and vendors are prohibited from absorbing the tax.[5] The taxpayer knows the amount of tax being paid and, theoretically, can evaluate the tax relative to the government services he or she receives. Although few citizens will undertake such an exercise, transparency represents an important component of sound tax policy and good government.[6]

Policy Issues: The Sales Tax under Siege

The levying of sales and use taxes in today's complex economy has raised significant policy issues. Some of these policy issues have plagued the tax for decades; others are the result of the evolving economic order. Cross-border transactions, constitutional limitations, failure to expand the tax base to services, and the advent of the age of electronic commerce have made the tax increasingly complex and call into question the tax's viability as a major source of revenue.

A Tax Base Riddled with Exemptions

In its purest form, the sales tax would apply to all final consumption (Mikesell 1998). In economic terms, no real rationale exists for excluding some types of consumption and taxing other types. Moreover, the stability of the tax, one of its primary virtues, is dependent on a broad base. Only if the tax applies to all, or most, personal consumption can states maintain steady levels of revenue through economic downturns. For a variety of reasons, however, barely half of all personal consumption is subject to tax in the United States. Many exemptions are granted for administrative reasons or to ease the regressivity of the tax. In addition, it is logistically difficult to impose the tax on many services, intangibles, and occasional sales. Although numerous exemptions make the tax more palatable politically, they pose serious problems for maintaining the integrity of the revenue stream.

Excessive exemption forces a state either to raise the sales tax rates or to forgo revenue. Sales tax revenue would probably double if all consumption were taxed. According to Mikesell (1998), food for home consumption alone constitutes about 20 percent of the sales tax base. Like other exemptions, not taxing food for home consumption, the policy in more than half the states, has a direct and substantial impact on state revenue.

The widespread granting of exemptions has another important consequence: higher tax rates on products and services subject to the tax (Mikesell 1992). A review of tax trends supports this assertion. The median sales tax rate rose from 2.7 percent in 1978 to 5.1 percent in 1993 (Due and Mikesell 1994). Since 1979, 21 percent of total sales tax revenue has been the result of rate increases (Fox 1997). Thirty-six states imposed higher rates during that time. These figures are astonishing because they occurred when antitax sentiment was sweeping the country. They also occurred during a time of unprecedented exemptions. This relationship is not coincidental. With more exemptions, rates must be increased on the remaining tax base simply to maintain existing levels of revenue.

Complexity

Another problem with the sales tax is that it has become increasingly complex. The widespread use of exemptions, in particular, complicates compliance and administration procedures, especially for multistate business transactions.

Multiple exemptions can also create confusion. Few individuals know exactly what products and services are or are not subject to tax. Some oft-cited examples of items that seem alike but are not taxed alike (out of the hundreds possible) illustrate the difficulty that taxpayers face: medicated dandruff shampoo is exempt, but regular shampoo is taxable; large marshmallows (considered a snack) may be taxable, but small marshmallows (considered food for home consumption) are exempt; and a pound of ham to be taken home is exempt, but a pound served with bread (considered a ready-to-eat meal) is taxable. In Florida, admissions to fresh-water fishing tournaments are exempt from tax, while admissions to salt-water fishing tournaments are taxable. So many exemptions exist, that even the government leaders who propose and support the exemptions often do not know what is or is not taxable (Brunori 2000a).

If a taxpayer cannot determine what is taxed, the benefits of transparency are essentially lost. For businesses, the cost of determining what is taxable is also significant. Anecdotal evidence suggests that owners of small businesses have a particularly difficult time complying with the tax. Because the vendor is liable for assessing the tax, many businesses collect taxes on items that in fact may be exempt.

Businesses operating in multiple jurisdictions find the plethora of different exemptions in each state even more vexing. The tax bases of most states imposing the sales tax vary widely. For example, of the 45 states taxing consumption, 18 tax transportation charges, 12 tax interest and finance charges, and 37 tax some form of telecommunications services. Moreover, food for home consumption is taxed in 19 states, but is exempt in 26 others. Some states exempt clothing; most states do not.

Of course, the rates and administrative procedures also vary among the 45 states imposing sales tax. Thus, multistate businesses must comply with different rates as well as a host of different rules. The inclusion of local option sales taxes compounds the problem. Many local governments in 33 states have the authority to impose sales and use taxes.

Technology has been used to ease some of the administrative burdens associated with complying with varying rate structures, filing requirements, and exemptions. Computer software can identify what products and services are subject to the sales tax, the rate of that tax, and the filing requirements.

Still, simplifying the sales tax is a crucial step in preserving its viability. Noted practitioners and scholars have repeatedly called on the states to devise a simpler, more efficient sales-tax system, especially for multistate transactions. One practitioner has called for better vendor compensation (to accurately reflect the costs of compliance), limitations on exemptions, wider dissemination of tax changes (through electronic bulletin boards), and greater uniformity in administration (Eggert 1995).

Remote Sales

One of the most daunting issues facing policymakers is the tax treatment of remote sales. Remote sales (the sale of goods and services through the mail, over the telephone, and on the Internet) have troubled policymakers for decades. But with the advent of the age of electronic commerce, the issue of remote sales has taken on new significance.

In the now well-known *Quill* decision,[7] the United States Supreme Court concluded that a state cannot compel a vendor to collect sales and use tax unless that vendor has a "physical presence" in the state.[8] Businesses that sell through mail-order catalogs, via telemarketing, or through Web sites often do not have a physical presence. Thus, they are not obligated to collect sales or use tax on the transaction and remit the proceeds to the state. Part of the difficulty in ensuring the success of taxing remote items is that sales-tax collection has always depended on the vendor. Because the vendor is liable for uncollected or unremitted tax, and since the state defrays some of the vendor's costs, compliance with the tax has traditionally been very high. Without vendor responsibility for collection, the sales tax could have trouble surviving.

The primary concern for the states, of course, is that uncollected taxes from remote sales will costs billions of dollars and require dramatic reforms, significant service reductions, or steep rate increases for other taxes. E-commerce will continue to grow. Indeed, some studies conclude that Internet retail sales alone will reach $108.0 billion by 2003, compared with sales of just $9.8 billion in 1998 (Duncan 1999).

The states fear that remote sales will add to the problem of an already eroding tax base.[9] And those concerns are justified. Conservative estimates show that the states lost about $170 million in sales tax revenue in 1998 (Cline and Neubig 1999). More significantly, 2003 projections for lost sales tax revenue range from $9.0 billion (Duncan 1999) to an astounding $20.1 billion (Bruce and Fox 2000).

In addition to the potential revenue loss, remote sales pose other political and policy problems for the states. By failing to tax remote sales, the states create horizontal inequities between traditional in-store purchases and transactions conducted via mail order or the Internet. In essence, the states have created an economic incentive to sell and purchase remotely—at the expense of traditional retailers. This, of course, creates significant political issues for state policymakers. Traditional retailers have protested the state tax system's tendency to place them at a competitive disadvantage in the marketplace (Brunori 2000b).

An Unfair Levy

Perhaps the oldest and strongest complaint about the sales tax is that it is regressive. Poorer individuals pay a larger percentage of their income in sales taxes than do middle- or upper-income people. For that reason, the sales tax has been called "the most unfair way for states to raise revenue" (Citizens for Tax Justice 1987, 9).

As income rises, the percentage of spending subject to sales tax falls. This relationship means that wealthier people save more in sales taxes than do the poor. They also spend more on services (legal, accounting, medical, etc.) that are generally not subject to sales tax. Poorer citizens, by contrast, spend a greater share of their income on taxable purchases, and thus pay a far larger percentage of their income in sales tax than do middle- or higher-income people.

Various studies have confirmed that the tax places a far greater burden on those at the lower end of the economic spectrum. A 1993 Minnesota study found that those earning in the bottom 10 percent paid 5.2 percent of their income in sales taxes, while those in the upper 10 percent paid just 1.3 percent (Due and Mikesell 1994). A Connecticut study in 1990 found that those earning under $5,000 paid 8.15 percent of their income in sales taxes, while those earning between $100,000 and $200,000 paid only 2.18 percent (Due and Mikesell 1994).[10]

Ironically, given its widespread use, the sales tax is viewed as regressive by state policymakers of both parties. Liberal politicians, of course, have long recognized the unfairness of the sales tax. But more conservative leaders are beginning to realize it as well. There are numerous examples of conservative political leaders calling for specific cuts in the sales tax rates for items deemed necessities—and citing the disproportionate burden placed on the poor (Morgan 2000).

Evidence of the perceived unfairness of the sales tax is that most states decide to exempt goods deemed necessities from the tax base on the belief that such taxes unfairly burden the poor. In most states, food, utilities, medicine, and, in some cases, clothing are exempt from sales tax to some extent.

The exemption of these necessities does alleviate some of the absolute tax burden on poorer citizens. The exemption for necessities, however, does not necessarily reduce the regressivity of the tax. Sales tax exemptions apply to the wealthy as well as the poor. And because the wealthy spend more on such necessities, their absolute taxable savings from such exemptions are even greater.

Moreover, the evidence suggests that sales tax exemptions for food, and perhaps other necessities, actually have a detrimental effect on the savings among the poor. When the state exempts food and other necessities from the tax, it usually raises rates on other items to replace the lost revenue (Bahl 1997). This is consistent with the notion that shrinking the tax base leads to higher rates on nonexempt goods and services, a fact often pointed out by sales tax scholars (Mikesell 1998). Because the poor often receive food stamps, a payment medium that exempts the overlying sale, they do not receive added relief from a food tax exemption.

The perceived unfairness of the tax has prompted state legislatures to proceed with tax relief measures such as back-to-school sales-tax holidays, which allow consumers to purchase specific products with no sales tax liability. Sales-tax holidays have been increasingly popular as politicians have sought ways to lessen the regressivity of the tax without fundamentally changing the tax and endangering billions of dollars in revenue.[11]

To ease the burden on poorer taxpayers, some states provide income tax credits or refunds on sales tax purchases. Taxpayers meeting certain income limits receive an income tax credit designed to lessen the regressivity of the sales tax. Theoretically, these credits are a much more effective means of alleviating the burdens on poorer taxpayers. It prevents further shrinkage of the tax base and does not allow wealthier taxpayers to benefit from a program designed specifically to help the poor.

Ultimately, most scholars, commentators, and policymakers have come to the same conclusion as Phares (1980): There is little question about the sales tax's regressive nature.

Taxation of Services

Most economists and scholars agree that the sales tax, as a tax on consumption, should be applied to consumer services (Fox 1998; Mikesell 1998). Yet most services are exempt in most states imposing the sales tax. The reason for the widespread exemptions is mostly historic. When sales and use taxes were first implemented, the exemption for services was not a significant issue. Services were a small segment of the national economy. Professional services (e.g., legal and medical) were thought to be impossible to tax for political reasons, while many nonprofessional services were thought to be impossible to tax for administrative reasons.

The exclusion of services in today's economy, however, results in a considerable loss of revenue for the states. Since 1979, services have risen from 47.4 percent to 57.5 percent of personal consumption. During that period, tangible goods have fallen by the same percentage (Fox 1997). While states have broadened the tax base to include more services in the past decade, many of the services that would yield the most revenue (e.g., health care, construction, legal, and accounting) go untaxed (Fox 1998).

There are several reasons for taxing services. First, no theoretical or economic reason exists for excluding services from the tax base. Services, after all, are consumed like tangible personal property. By exempting services, the tax system discriminates against taxable goods. Thus, persons who consume *goods* bear a greater tax burden than similarly situated persons who consume *services*.

Taxing services will likely make the sales tax less regressive. Wealthier people have and will continue to spend a greater percentage of their income on services. Therefore, taxing services would likely improve vertical equity.[12]

Second, taxing services would broaden the tax base and provide some opportunity to raise more revenue or reduce rates. With a great percentage of consumption sales now exempt from taxation, broadening the base would result in significant additional revenue for the states. Indeed, aggregate sales tax revenue would more than double if all services consumed by individuals were subject to sales tax.

Third, taxing services would lead to a more elastic tax base. One of the virtues of the sales tax is that it is a stable source of revenue. It neither rises nor falls as quickly as personal income. But that stability is dependent on a broad base, and it is challenged when large segments of potentially taxable consumables are removed from the tax base. The sales tax base is not nearly as stable as it was designed to be, or could be. And the most viable policy for broadening the base is to tax services.

There are, of course, several disadvantages to taxing services. Taxation of services would inevitably lead to greater sales tax burdens on businesses—which account for a significant majority of service purchases. As discussed below, business inputs should not be taxed under a pure consumption tax because the sales tax itself would then be embedded in the ultimate cost to consumers.

Taxation of services would also increase administrative and compliance costs for both the government and taxpayers. Unlike products, many services do not leave a record of production and inventory. Tracking the quantity and value of services rendered is a daunting task.

In addition to these disadvantages, political obstacles have deterred states from taxing services. Most professional services that would generate substantial revenue are provided by economic interests with significant political power. Lawyers, accountants, doctors, dentists, and financial advisors can be expected to oppose vigorously any efforts to tax the services that they provide. For example, in 1987 the state of Florida tried to broaden its tax base to include many services, but the political opposition was impossible to overcome.[13] However, three states—Hawaii, South Dakota, and New Mexico—have successfully levied sales taxes on most services.

Taxation of Business Inputs

Ideally, the sales and use tax should not be levied on consumption of business inputs (Fox 1997; Mikesell 1998). Although many business purchases are exempt from the tax (e.g., purchases for resale, ingredients for a manufactured product, and sales of machinery), a significant portion of business inputs are taxed. An early and oft-cited study found that 41 percent of the sales tax was paid directly by businesses (Ring 1989).

Serious problems can result when a state subjects business inputs to sales taxation. From a theoretical perspective, the tax was designed as a levy on *personal consumption*—which leaves no basis for taxing products or services before consumption occurs. When business inputs are subject to tax, the ultimate product price will contain the tax. Thus, consumers are taxed on the tax itself, an effect known as pyramiding. This outcome was probably unintended by policymakers.

Moreover, the additional tax is effectively hidden from those with the burden of paying it. As noted earlier, one of the advantages of the sales tax is its transparency. Taxing business inputs raises revenue in a manner that obscures the party that bears the burden of paying the tax.

Taxation of business inputs may also encourage vertical integration, which is not always the best economic choice for businesses. Vertical integration occurs when a business determines that producing a needed service or product is more efficient than purchasing it from an unrelated party. Because the sales tax often represents a significant cost of purchase, especially in cases where the costs cannot be fully passed on to customers, taxing business inputs could lead to increased vertical integration. Thus, the principle that taxes should remain as neutral as possible when it comes to influencing business decisions is largely ignored in cases where business inputs are subject to sales tax.

But eliminating the sales tax on business purchases—though a theoretically sound idea—will be difficult. Sales taxation of business purchases raises billions of dollars for state treasuries. Exempting all business purchases would create serious budgetary shortfalls, necessitating either increases in other taxes or cutbacks in services. Without a comprehensive tax reform effort identifying additional revenue sources, eliminating business purchases from taxation would be problematic. Comprehensive reform efforts should entail expanding the sales tax base to include services while reducing the tax on business inputs.

Moreover, the sales tax on business purchases is politically attractive. There is widespread support for the taxation of business consumption, especially when the alternative is to tax wages or personal consumption. In this regard, providing widespread tax cuts for businesses in the name of sound tax policy would not be politically feasible. More importantly, the sales tax on businesses, although passed on to the consumer in most cases, is largely hidden from view. This invisibility is a problem from an accountability standpoint (the public is unaware of the tax). But from a political standpoint, it is generally considered preferable. Furthermore, a significant portion—and in some states a very significant share—of the tax burden falls on out-of-state business.

Despite the political opposition to eliminating the tax on business inputs, the point may be moot. More and more business purchases will likely become exempt from the sales tax in the future through exemptions designed to promote economic development. State legislatures have steadily increased the amount of business exemptions in recent years in an effort to spur economic development. While the granting of tax exemptions is fraught with policy problems, it may serve to minimize the taxation of business inputs.

Federal Sales Tax

In recent years, an old debate about possibly replacing the federal income tax with some type of consumption tax has been revived. Policymakers in Washington have discussed various national sales tax proposals.[14] The wisdom of adopting a national sales tax is outside the scope of this work; however, it is important to note some of the problems that a national sales tax could create within the states.

One problem is that a federal sales tax would seriously curtail the states' ability to collect their own sales taxes. The states have considerable autonomy within the limitations of the Commerce Clause to impose the sales tax. Thus far, the federal government's decision to refrain from taxing consumption (except for various excises) has added to that autonomy. If the federal government adopted a national sales tax, the size of the tax (according to policymakers' proposed rates) would severely hamper states' ability to raise revenue with a separate tax.

Moreover, a federal consumption tax would likely result in national rules governing state tax bases and rates. These restrictions would limit the states' ability to design their tax systems to meet the needs of their citizens and business communities.

These problems, while important to note, are not likely to materialize any time soon. The economic fortunes of the late 1990s have eroded support for major federal tax reform. The large federal surpluses projected in the near term make such reform unlikely in the early part of this century.

Future Policy: What It Takes to Save the Sales Tax

The sales tax is not in danger of disappearing, at not least in the foreseeable future. The tax raises far too much revenue, and income or other taxes cannot easily replace that revenue. The question is whether the sales tax will continue to play a dominant, or even a significant, role in state public finance. Many noted scholars and commentators have questioned the viability of the tax (Fox 1998; Mikesell 1998; Murray 1997). The sales tax base continues to shrink as political leaders exempt more consumer goods and services from the tax. Consumer spending also continues to tilt toward services and intellectual property, which are generally not subject to sales tax. The most pressing issue, of course, is the advent of electronic commerce and the problem of taxing remote sales. The amount of goods and services sold electronically will severely test state sales tax regimes.

Declines in sales tax revenue pose a serious problem for the states. Substantial reductions in sales tax revenue will force state political leaders either to find alternative sources of revenue or to reduce public services. Few alternative sources of revenue are available. Political and economic pressures prevent increasing business tax burdens. There is little room for growth in excise taxes and user fees. The only viable revenue alternative for many states is the personal income tax. Increased reliance on the income tax, however, will likely lead to serious erosion of public support for that tax. Given states' revenue needs, the sales tax base must be strengthened. Several policy options can help state legislators accomplish that goal.

Broaden the Tax Base

First, the states must take steps to broaden the tax base. They could accomplish this objective by taxing all tangible personal property and services purchased by consumers. Virtually all tangible personal property is already subject to the tax; items deemed necessities should be added back to the tax base.

The exemptions for necessities are aimed at alleviating tax burdens on the poor. But the evidence is mixed, at best, as to whether these exemptions accomplish their goal. Moreover, such exemptions cost the states substantial revenue because middle- and upper-income individuals enjoy the exemptions as well. There are more efficient and effective means of assisting the poor, including refundable income tax credits and other direct payments.

Politically, ending the exemption for necessities would be difficult. But taxing exemptions could result in lower sales tax rates (for all taxpayers) and more effective assistance to the poor. Equally important, compromise might be reached on those grounds.

To broaden the tax base, states should also tax all services. There is no economic justification for excluding any services from a tax on consumption. Yet, although many services are taxed, professional services are generally exempt. In today's business environment, professional services constitute a large segment of the economy. Including services in the tax base would result in a significant increase in revenue. In turn, it would allow legislators to lower tax rates, perhaps significantly, on tangible personal property.

Previous attempts to expand the tax base in this manner have met significant opposition and have ultimately failed. The main opposition has come from politically powerful professional service providers (attorneys, doctors, and accountants). These groups could be expected to oppose future attempts at taxing services. Still, there may be opportunities for compromise. For example, business purchases of professional services should be exempt from the sales tax. In addition, broadening the tax base to include services could be coupled with significant reductions in other tax rates, including those on personal income. As advocated by William Fox (1998), a noted scholar and longtime observer of the tax, taxation of services should be approached aggressively.

Tax Remote Sales

States must find a way to tax remote sales. More specifically, they must find a way to require out-of-state vendors to collect the tax. Allowing

mail-order or electronic purchases to escape taxation is unfair to traditional retailers, and it distorts the market by providing a tax advantage to
online or mail-order shoppers and businesses. It also results in significant lost revenue for the states, necessitating higher tax rates on in-state
purchases and other taxes.

States have three options for successfully taxing remote sales. First,
the states could challenge the Supreme Court's decision in *Quill*, which
requires a physical presence in the state for taxing jurisdiction. But nothing suggests that the Court would entertain such a challenge. Therefore,
a judicial solution to the problem of taxing remote sales is unlikely.

Second, the states could seek a legislative solution. Congress has the
power under the Commerce Clause to require remote vendors to collect
and remit sales taxes. Soon after the *Quill* decision, Senator Dale
Bumpers (D-AR) introduced his Fairness to Main Street Act, which
would have required remote sellers to collect sales and use tax on all
transactions. Bumpers introduced the measure in three consecutive congressional sessions. But strong lobbying on the part of mail-order companies, represented by the Direct Marketing Association, prevented
Bumpers' proposals from even coming to a vote (Brunori 2000b). More
recently, Senator Byron L. Dorgan (D-ND), sponsored a similar bill, the
Internet Tax Moratorium and Equity Act. Opposition from the high-
technology industry, however, will make a legislative solution to the
problem of taxing remote sales difficult.

An agreement between industry and the states that devises a mechanism for collecting sales tax on remote purchase is the most promising
option. Representatives from the states and the business community
have been discussing this possibility for several years. Efforts include the
Streamlined Sales Tax Project, which is designed to alleviate the complexity and resulting compliance costs for business, while protecting the
states' sales tax base. If the concerns of the business community can be
addressed through simplification, the problems of remote sales have a
good chance of being solved.

Stop Taxing Business Inputs

Because sales tax is meant as a tax on consumption, economists and
public finance experts agree that sales taxes should not be imposed on
business purchases. Yet much of the states' sales tax revenue is collected
from such purchases. To truly reform the sales tax into a consumption
tax, business inputs should be excluded from the tax base. Although this

reform runs counter to the overarching goal of broadening the tax base, it addresses an important problem in imposing a hidden tax on consumers. Taxes on business inputs, while attractive politically, are generally passed on to consumers in the form of higher prices.

As noted in chapter 4, political leaders wish to obscure taxes and will thus tend to tax business inputs. This bias would need to be overcome by those truly interested in reform, which may be easier than it sounds. Businesses would surely support elimination of the sales tax on inputs. Similarly, individual consumers would likely favor such reform if they understood that they are already bearing the burden of these taxes. Even if rates on other consumer purchases increased, buyers, on net, would be paying the same amount of tax.

These policies amount to significant reforms of the existing sales tax structure. They will all face serious political opposition. Accomplishing even a few will be difficult. But only significant reform can ensure survival of the sales tax as a major source of revenue for the states.

NOTES

1. Unless explicitly stated, references to sales taxes include use taxes as well as retailer occupation and privilege taxes, since there is no economic difference between them. For an in-depth discussion of these variations on the sales tax, see Hellerstein and Hellerstein (1999). Unless otherwise noted, all state and use tax data are for 1998 and are from the U.S. Census Bureau (2000).
2. The 10 states that are most dependent on the sales tax are Florida, Tennessee, Washington, Texas, South Dakota, New Mexico, Arizona, Nevada, Hawaii, and Mississippi. Not surprisingly, six of these states do not tax personal income.
3. Information on the costs of administration with respect to small business are from author interviews with state revenue department officials.
4. While no public records detailing use tax compliance are available, the author estimates that less than 5 percent of individuals with use tax liability comply with the law.
5. For an in-depth discussion of the rules concerning separately stating the tax, see Due and Mikesell (1994).
6. However, as noted later in this chapter, the benefits of transparency are not apparent when states impose sales taxes on business inputs. Indeed, much of the burden of the sales tax is disguised by the taxation of business inputs.
7. *Quill v. North Dakota*, 504 U.S. 298 (1992).
8. While "physical presence" is now routinely used to describe the nexus requirement, the term has never been defined by the Supreme Court (Mines 1997).
9. Bruce and Fox (2000) found that the sales tax base as a percentage of personal income fell from 51.4 percent in 1979 to 42.8 percent in 1998.

10. The question of whether the sales tax is regressive is subject to some debate. If annual income is used as the measure of wealth, then the tax is clearly regressive. If, however, lifetime income is used as the measure of wealth, the sales tax is thought to be proportional in its distributional effects (Metcalf 1993; Zodrow 1999). Because taxes are paid out of current income, however, a sales tax that may be proportional over the long run is of little solace to poorer taxpayers.

11. For a discussion on the wisdom and efficacy of sales-tax holidays, see Brunori (2000c).

12. Taxing some services, such as repairs, might actually have a regressive effect because poor individuals are more likely to seek repairs than to purchase new automobiles, home appliances, and other high-priced items.

13. The Florida legislature passed a law broadening the sales tax base to include advertising and other services. The resulting political opposition led to an almost immediate reversal of the policy.

14. The federal tax reform proposals calling for levies on consumption include the so-called U.S.A. Tax, proposed by former Senator Sam Nunn (D-GA) and Senator Pete Dominici (R-NM), and a national retail sales tax proposed by Senator Richard G. Lugar (R-IN) (Faber 1998).

REFERENCES

Advisory Commission on Intergovernmental Affairs. 1993. *Changing Public Attitudes on Government and Taxes.* Washington, D.C.: Advisory Commission on Intergovernmental Affairs.

Bahl, Roy. 1997. "Does a Food Exemption Lead to Higher State Sales Tax Rates?" *State Tax Notes* (January 5): 27–30.

Bruce, Donald, and William F. Fox. 2000. "E-Commerce in the Context of Declining State Sales Tax Bases." Knoxville, Tenn.: Center for Business and Economic Research.

Brunori, David. 1999a. "Interview: John L. Mikesell on the Present and Future of the Sales Tax." *State Tax Notes* (November 22): 1364–1373.

———. 1999b. "Sales Tax Holidays: Real Relief or Political Gimmicks?" *State Tax Notes* (December 6): 1521–1522.

———. 2000a. "Random Musings on the Sales Tax." *State Tax Notes* (March 6): 759–760.

———. 2000b. "Mad on Main Street: Retailers and Internet Taxation." *State Tax Notes* (September 18): 765–767.

Citizens for Tax Justice. 1987. *The Sorry State of State Taxes.* Washington, D.C.: Citizens for Tax Justice.

Cline, Robert J., and Thomas S. Neubig. 1999. "The Sky Is Not Falling: Why State and Local Revenues Were Not Significantly Impacted by the Internet in 1998." *State Tax Notes* (July 5): 43–46.

Cole, Richard L., and John Kincaid. 2000. "Public Opinion and American Federalism: Perspectives on Taxes, Spending, and Trust—An ACIR Update." *Publius* 30 (winter/spring): 189–201.

Due, John, and John Mikesell. 1994. *Sales Taxation*. Washington, D.C.: Urban Institute Press.

Duncan, Harley. 1999. "State Revenue Losses from E-Commerce Underestimated." *State Tax Notes* (July 26): 245–247.

Eggert, Wayne. 1995. "State and Local Sales/Use and Property Tax Simplification—A Call to Action." *State Tax Notes* (November 13): 1411–1419.

Faber, Peter. 1998. "Effect of Federal Tax Reform on State and Local Governments." *State Tax Notes* (March 16): 826–831.

Federation of Tax Administrators (FTA). 1999. "State Tax Collections by State." Http://www.taxadmin.org/fta/rate.

Fox, William. 1997. "Importance of the Sales Tax in the 21st Century." In *Sales Taxation in the 21st Century*, edited by Matthew N. Murray and William Fox (348). Westport, Conn.: Praeger.

———. 1998. "Can the Sales Tax Survive a Future Like Its Past?" In *The Future of State Taxation*, edited by David Brunori (33–48). Washington, D.C.: Urban Institute Press.

Hellerstein, Walter, and Jerome Hellerstein. 1999. *State Taxation*. New York: Warren Gorham and Lamont.

Metcalf, Gilbert. 1993. "The Lifetime Incidence of State and Local Sales Taxes." National Bureau of Economic Research, Working Paper 4252.

Mikesell, John. 1992. "State Tax Policy in a Changing Economy." *Public Budgeting and Finance* (spring): 75–101.

———. 1996. "Should Grocery Food Purchases Bear a Sales Tax Burden?" *State Tax Notes* 11 (September 9): 751–754.

———. 1998. "The Future of American Sales and Use Taxation." In *The Future of State Taxation*, edited by David Brunori (15–32). Washington, D.C.: Urban Institute Press.

Mines, Paull. 1997. "Conversing with Professor Hellerstein: Electronic Commerce and Nexus Propel Sales and Use Tax Reform." *Tax Law Review* 52 (4): 581.

Morgan, Ann Marie. 2000. "Virginia Governor: Food Tax, Car Tax Cuts Will Continue." *State Tax Notes* (August 28): 554.

Murray, Mathew. 1998. "Moving the Retail Sales Tax to a Retail Tax." In *Sales Taxation in the 21st Century*, edited by Matthew N. Murray and William Fox (193–203). Westport, Conn.: Praeger.

Phares, Donald. 1980. *Who Pays the State and Local Taxes?* Cambridge, Mass.: Oelgaschlager, Gunn, and Hain.

Ring, Raymond. 1989. "The Proportion of Consumers' and Producers' Goods in the General Sales Tax." *National Tax Journal* 44 (June): 167–179.

U.S. Census Bureau. 2000. "Federal, State, and Local Governments: 1998 State Government Finance Data." Http://www.census.gov/govs/www/state98.html.

Zodrow, George. 1999. *State Sales and Income Taxes*. College Station, Tex.: Texas A&M University Press.

6

State Personal
Income Taxes

*Nothing hurts more than having to pay an income tax, unless it is
not having to pay an income tax.*

—Thomas Dewar

Forty-one states and the District of Columbia impose a broad-based
personal income tax. Alaska, Texas, Florida, Washington, Nevada,
South Dakota, and Wyoming do not impose any levies on personal
income. Tennessee and New Hampshire tax certain dividend, interest,
and capital gains income, but they do not tax wages and salaries.

The personal income tax plays a vital role in financing state government, and accounts for about one-third of total state tax revenue in the
United States. It has become increasingly important over the past several
decades. In 1950, the personal income tax accounted for only 9.3 percent
of total state tax revenue. By 1970, that figure had risen to 19 percent. By
1998, the tax constituted 34 percent of total state tax revenue and had
become the single largest source of state tax revenue, surpassing the sales
tax for the first time.[1] The emergence of the income tax as the single
largest source of revenue for the states is significant because some large
states (e.g., Texas and Florida) do not tax personal income.

Part of the growth in the income tax is attributable to the enactment
of income tax laws in Pennsylvania, Rhode Island, and Ohio in 1971;
New Jersey in 1976; and Connecticut in 1991. In addition, the booming
economy of the mid- and late 1990s produced an explosion in personal
income. The rapid growth of the high-technology industry, the proliferation of employee stock options, and an escalating real estate market
helped fuel this explosion. In the late 1990s, many states experienced

record-breaking budget surpluses because of the dramatic increase in personal income tax revenue.

A large part of the growth, however, is also attributable to the rise in restrictions on other types of taxes (Brunori 1998). For example, consumption, business, excise, and other taxes have been limited by political, economic, and technological changes. The personal income tax has remained relatively free from many of the pressures that have plagued other taxes.

In states that levy a personal income tax, however, there is a decided political bias against personal income taxes when they are considered with other types of levies. Paradoxically, the income tax faces the most opposition from state legislators, despite producing tremendous amounts of revenue and enjoying widespread public support. Part of that opposition is grounded in the belief that people's wages should not be taxed. Part of the resistance also reflects the belief that income taxes deter economic growth. Political leaders often believe that income taxes place their states at a competitive disadvantage.

In the nine states without a general personal income tax, there is a tradition of profound opposition to taxing income. And while the issue of adopting a levy on personal income has been hotly debated in several states in recent years, particularly in New Hampshire and Tennessee, almost insurmountable obstacles to adoption of the tax exist in most states that do not tax income.

Successful opposition to a personal income tax likely persists because these states have other significant sources of income. In Washington, South Dakota, Texas, Alaska, and Wyoming, various severance taxes from natural resources (e.g., timber, petroleum, and minerals) account for large percentages of tax revenue. Nevada and Florida rely heavily on revenue raised from the tourism industry to support their public services.[2]

Still, despite some states' decision not to tax income, the personal income tax has become the dominant source of state revenue. Many state tax scholars believe that this trend will continue (Brunori 1999a; Brunori 1999b).

Success of the Tax

A decade of economic expansion and the adoption of the income tax by five states have resulted in more income taxes being collected than ever in the past. Several features of the tax itself, however, have also contributed to its growing importance to state budgets.

Public Acceptance

Most notably, the public has expressed little dissatisfaction with the state income tax. Opinion polls have routinely indicated that the public rates the tax as the most acceptable form of taxation (Cole and Kincaid 2000; Dearborn 1993). For that reason, politicians and policymakers have been under no serious political pressure to eliminate the tax or to decrease its importance as a source of revenue. That cannot be said of other state and local taxes. For many years the property tax spurred citizen revolts across the country.

The public's acceptance of the state income tax contrasts sharply with its attitude toward the federal income tax, which along with the property tax is one of America's least-favorite levies. The public's opinions about the federal tax have often figured in the outcome of national elections. Presidents Jimmy Carter, Ronald Reagan, and George Bush all made federal income tax policy an important part of their ultimately victorious campaigns. Dissatisfaction with the federal income tax has also given rise to periodic calls by congressional leaders for significant reform and even repeal of the tax.

On the whole, the state income tax has not created public resentment or caused political turmoil. And while an increasing number of states have adopted the tax, very few have made serious efforts to eliminate the tax once it is in place. Even statewide political campaigns, with some exceptions, do not typically focus on state personal income tax issues.[3]

Political concerns over the personal income tax do, of course, occasionally arise. As noted in chapter 4, the New Jersey's gubernatorial race between Jim Florio and Christine Todd Whitman in 1993 was decided almost exclusively on the issue of personal income taxes. Another noteworthy example occurred after Connecticut adopted an income tax for the first time in 1991. Thousands of citizens flocked to Hartford, the state's capital, and burned in effigy Governor Lowell Weicker (I), who had led the enactment of the tax. The protests were short-lived. Although Weicker chose not to seek reelection and several lawmakers who supported the tax were later defeated, succeeding legislatures failed to overturn the tax.

In most cases, however, the state income tax has proved to be politically acceptable to state residents. Even efforts to repeal the tax have not gained much momentum. In 1998, the Kansas Public Policy Institute, a conservative research organization, recommended that the state phase out the graduated income tax as a way to stimulate the economy. Governor Bill Graves (R) rejected the proposal, noting that Kansas needed to balance its sources of revenue. He cited the unfairness of funding public services solely through consumption taxes, a surprising stance for a conservative politician (Courtwright 1998). In the past decade, a time of record-setting budget surpluses, Republicans and Democrats alike have generally looked for other ways than eliminating the personal income tax to reduce tax burdens.

Consistent Performance

The personal income tax was once seen as an unstable source of income for the states. Many public finance experts believed that while revenue would increase rapidly under good economic conditions, it would decline with equal rapidity in leaner times (Gold 1991). Recent history, however, has shown that the state personal income tax revenue has grown immensely through good times and bad. Between 1980 and 1993, a period when America suffered severe economic hardships, revenue from state individual income tax grew by an astonishing 204 percent (Megna 1997).

Given that growth, the unprecedented increase in state personal income tax is not surprising. During the late 1990s, when many states experienced record budget surpluses and were engaged in wide-scale tax cutting, every state chose to reduce effective personal income tax burdens for its citizens. Still, revenue from the personal income tax grew from $125 billion in 1995 to $161 billion in 1998.

Low Rates/Federal Deductibility

Most states impose relatively low rates, especially compared with income tax rates set by the federal government. In 1998, according to the Federation of Tax Administrators (FTA), the highest income tax rate for most states was below 6 percent. In that year, only four states (California, Hawaii, Montana, and Oregon) had marginal rates over 9 percent, according to FTA. The states with the highest marginal rates also offered the most generous exemptions and standard deductions to ease the tax burden on low- and middle-income taxpayers.

The federal income tax may help promote the public's acceptance of the state tax in another way. For Americans who itemize their federal tax returns, the state personal income tax is deductible for federal income tax purposes. Although only a small percentage of Americans itemize their federal returns, this group is one of the most politically active of society. The benefit of this deduction thus applies to the people who are most likely to show their appreciation at the voting booth.

The state income tax also meets the criterion of transparency. The tax is highly visible mainly because it is automatically withheld from taxpayers' paychecks. Taxpayers can easily determine the amount being withheld and evaluate the services they receive. (High visibility can also be a detriment; large tax payments, either withheld or paid directly, can create "sticker shock" and lead to public dissatisfaction.)

Like the sales tax, the state income tax also does not generally produce dissatisfaction, because of the relatively low rates imposed by the states. The small percentage of the average person's pay withheld for state income tax purposes pales when compared with the amount withheld for federal income taxes. Taxpayers wondering where their money goes will more likely focus on the larger percentage withheld by the federal government.

Modest Compliance and Administrative Burdens

State income taxes, while more complicated for individuals than consumption and property taxes, entail relatively modest compliance burdens for taxpayers and relatively light administrative duties for government. This is especially true in comparison with state corporate income and federal income taxes. Because most Americans are subject to state income tax withholding, the tax is largely collected and remitted to the state long before returns must be filed. Moreover, because of withholding requirements, the vast majority of taxpayers need to file only one return per year. With the exception of a handful of states where the law is more complicated and for individuals with unusually complicated transaction records, completing the state personal income tax return is not complicated or time-consuming.

Accounting procedures also help ease the administrative burdens and facilitate compliance to the tax. According to the FTA, 27 states use federal adjusted gross income to determine state taxable income. In these states, taxpayers prepare their federal returns and simply transfer the adjusted gross income amount to their state returns. Seven states use federal taxable income as the starting point for calculating state income tax liability but require some additional calculations (FTA 1999). In 1999, three states (Rhode Island, Vermont, and North Dakota) use a percentage of federal tax to calculate personal income tax liability. These states' taxpayers must determine their federal income tax liability and pay a percentage of that amount to the state. In 1999, only four states (Alabama, Arkansas, Pennsylvania, and Mississippi) did not use any part of the federal tax scheme for determining state income taxes (FTA 1999). But even in those states, while additions and subtractions are often made to the federal income amount, these changes are usually inconsequential.

The tax is even more attractive to administrators. State revenue departments spend very little time monitoring compliance with the income tax, largely because of the widespread withholding of state income taxes. Before the end of each fiscal year, most of the personal income tax has already been collected. In addition, because most taxpayers must use federal income as the starting point for determining state income tax liability, they have a strong motive for paying the full amount of the tax. State tax evasion almost always requires federal tax evasion as well.

Cooperation between the states and the Internal Revenue Service (IRS) helps ease administration of the tax. Almost every state has entered into an agreement with the IRS to share information. In cases where the IRS makes an adjustment to federal adjusted gross income, it promptly informs the state revenue department of the change. States, of course, engage in some audit activities in the area of personal income tax. Most, however, can afford to limit their administration and enforcement activities to questions of residency, unreported income, and return errors.

In many respects, state revenue departments would have essentially delegated personal income tax auditing to the federal government. Allowing the federal government to audit and enforce the personal income tax laws probably adds to the public's acceptance of state income taxation.

High Level of Fairness

One of the most powerful justifications for the personal income tax is that it is viewed by many as the most equitable of all state taxes (NCSL

1992). As noted in chapter 2, most observers view fairness in terms of progressivity. Others believe that proportional taxation is the key to fairness. But virtually everyone agrees that a fair tax system minimizes regressivity. The personal income tax is widely viewed as the most progressive of all state taxes. It is certainly more progressive than general sales and excise taxes, the other major sources of tax revenue.[4]

All states impose income taxes that are at least mildly progressive because they exempt some portion of income up to a certain amount. Even Pennsylvania, which has a flat 2.8 percent tax on all income and no deductions or exemptions, forgives the income tax for persons with income at or below the poverty line (Bright 1998).

The progressivity of the income tax systems varies widely from state to state. Thirty-six states use a graduated rate schedule, which taxes income at higher marginal rates as income increases. The graduated personal income tax tends to be progressive. Six states (Massachusetts, Colorado, Illinois, Indiana, Mississippi, and Pennsylvania) use a single flat rate on all income, which creates a more regressive system. This regressivity, however, is typically addressed through exemptions and deductions.

It should be noted, however, that the state income tax as a whole has become decidedly less progressive over the past quarter-century (Lav and Gold 1993). Widespread tax cuts, deductions, credits, and exclusions have narrowed the tax base and reduced the relative tax burden on the wealthiest taxpayers. In the 1990s, most state adjustments to the income tax narrowed the base and benefited the wealthy more than the poor. For example, in 1996 eight states lowered their personal income tax rates, while six states increased their standard deductions (Mackey 1996). Both of these types of policies lessen the progressivity of the tax.

Still, the income tax satisfies the requirements of vertical equity far more than any other state tax. Even in states with flat rates, enough income is exempt from the tax so that lower-income persons are removed from the tax rolls. Thus, even in these states the tax is levied on a somewhat progressive basis.

The tax does less well in satisfying the requirements of horizontal equity. Optimally, the tax should be imposed on a broad base with few deductions, exclusions, or exemptions. That ideal, of course, is never the case. A plethora of deductions, exemptions, and exclusions granted every year are designed to benefit veterans, the elderly, families with small children, homeowners, and others.

The failure to achieve horizontal equity illustrates one of the personal income tax's most significant problems. Overreliance on the tax leads to political pressure to provide more exclusions, deductions, and credits and, in turn, to a narrowing of the tax base (Cline 1986). States then must raise rates to collect sufficient revenue. Despite widespread calls from economists and commentators to limit the use of tax preferences, state political leaders have been unable to resist the temptation to provide income tax breaks. Most relief goes to groups with widespread public and political support, making the types of reforms needed to curb tax preferences extremely difficult to attain.

Policy Issues

Although the state personal income tax's importance has increased over the last 30 years, the tax raises several policy concerns for legislators and administrators. These concerns will become even more pronounced if the tax continues to grow relative to other levies.

Political Pressure

The effect of antitax politics on state income taxes is one of the most serious problems facing state governments. While the tax has grown in relative importance as a source of revenue (as incomes have grown), legislators often do not turn to the tax when looking for ways to generate new revenue. Rather, state legislatures tend to favor adjusting less progressive taxes.

When states must raise additional revenue, they are far more likely to increase sales and use taxes by either broadening the base or enacting rate hikes than to increase personal income taxes. Conversely, states that can afford to reduce tax burdens are far more likely to cut personal income taxes through exemptions/deductions or rate adjustments than they are to cut the more regressive consumption taxes (NCSL 2000).

The tendency to rely on personal income taxes to raise revenue largely reflects political and public perceptions. Political leaders widely believe that income taxation deters economic growth and that relatively high income tax burdens place a state at a competitive disadvantage relative to other states. Political leaders primarily concerned with economic growth and job creation have demonstrated a strong bias against policies that hinder—or give the perception of hindering—these two goals (see chapter 2). Many political leaders view personal income taxes as detrimental to economic growth. Other levies, such as those on consumption or property, have never suffered from this perception. Thus, when faced with the choice of raising revenue through income or other types of taxes, state legislators usually choose to raise personal income taxes.

This perception may continue because so few states conduct incidence studies on the effects of their tax policy decisions (Johnson and Lav 1997). Legislators rarely have analyses to consult when making tax policy decisions. Without a formal, nonpartisan explanation of who pays and who benefits from certain types of taxes, the true effects of pending tax legislation are often lost on the ultimate decisionmakers. Noting that a tax is regressive is not nearly as powerful as, for example, showing that a person who earns $20,000 will pay 3 percent of his or her salary in taxes, while a person earning $200,000 will pay less than 1 percent. Some public interest organizations—in particular the Institute for Taxation and Economic Policy and the Center on Budget and Policy Priorities—analyze tax proposals in select states. These studies often shed welcome light on the inequities of state tax policy. The majority of state legislators, however, make tax policy decisions without the benefit of detailed evaluations of who will ultimately pay.

The lack of knowledge of the specific burdens and benefits is part of a larger problem. Most legislators have some idea that sales taxes are generally regressive and that income taxes are generally progressive. Legislators, however, always have an eye toward helping—or at least not harming—those who wield economic power in the state. Political support, campaign contributions, and networks of voters are at stake. The general lack of information about who pays and benefits and to what degree gives those with powerful economic interests greater leverage in the decision-making process. The public generally does not know that these cuts may be unfair. Furthermore, state politicians who favor sales tax cuts often do not have data to support their case.

More cynically perhaps, legislators might intentionally decide to reduce income tax burdens knowing that the wealthier segments of society will benefit most. Wealthier individuals are more likely to vote—and to contribute to political campaigns.

Lack of Inflation Indexing

One of the least-discussed shortcomings of the state income tax is that most states do not index tax brackets or exemptions to inflation. As of 1999, only 16 states indexed either brackets or exemptions to inflation. In those states without indexing, inflation pushes taxpayers into higher income brackets (or decreases the value of their exemptions) every year. Thus, their tax liability increases at a faster rate than their real income.

The lack of inflation indexing creates a more regressive tax system overall. Eventually, it can lead to a system that taxes citizens with incomes at or below the poverty line. One study found that in 1996, 23 states taxed families below the poverty line and, incredibly, 6 states taxed families with income less than one-half the poverty line (Liebschutz 1998). Periods of high inflation, such as the 1970s, magnify the problems posed by a lack of indexing.

The failure to index brackets and exemptions runs counter to the philosophy of the personal income tax—that individuals who earn more should pay proportionately more in taxes. It also amounts to a tax increase without the benefit of legislative debate or approval. Most important, the public is unlikely to sanction a tax on the income of persons living well below the poverty line.

Changing Demographics and Compensation

Another little-discussed policy issue is the rapidly changing demographics of the country. The American population is aging, a development that will slow the growth of the personal income tax. By 2039, 20 percent of Americans will be 65 years or older, compared with 16 percent in 1993 (NCSL 1993). As Americans grow older, they earn less taxable income and are eligible for more tax preferences.

Another change that will affect the state personal income tax is the way Americans are compensated for their work. Working Americans are increasingly receiving fringe benefits that are not subject to federal income tax. This trend could slow the growth of state personal income tax. Between 1970 and 1990, fringe benefits—such as health insurance, pretax contributions to pension plans, and flexible spending accounts—have grown from 8.0 percent to 11.7 percent of total compensation (NCSL 1993). The aging population and the growth in fringe benefits will not affect the public's acceptance of the state personal income tax. They could, however, curtail the growth of a tax that has the best potential to help meet future revenue needs.

Federal Income Tax Changes

In recent years, national political leaders have proposed dramatic revisions to the way the federal government collects revenue. Many of these proposals have called for the elimination of the federal income tax and the adoption of some type of national consumption tax.

Eliminating, or even significantly altering, the federal income tax would create serious problems for the states. As noted, most states base their tax systems to some extent on the federal income tax. Without federal conformity, much of the ease of compliance and administration that has led to the success of state income taxes would disappear (Sheffrin 1996). Moreover, much of the political acceptance of the tax would likely evaporate once the state income tax became the only levy withheld from pay.

In one sense, the states would enjoy more autonomy and discretion if the federal government did not tax personal income. At the same time, however, the increased administrative and compliance costs have led observers to conclude that the state income tax could not survive repeal of the federal income tax (Bucks 1995). The booming economy of the late 1990s has lessened the political pressure to eliminate or dramatically change the federal income tax. The issue tends to reappear, however, during economic downturns.

Outlook for the Personal Income Tax: Guarding against Overreliance

The state personal income tax will continue to be an important source of revenue for state governments. Its importance is likely to grow as we enter the 21st century. Indeed, the tax is likely to dominate state public finance in the next half-century the way that the sales tax dominated the past half-century. The tax will remain an important source of revenue because it is relatively easy to administer, has demonstrated consistent growth, and is widely accepted by the citizens.

But its success perpetuates other problems of state finance. The personal income tax has resulted in dramatic revenue growth for the states. And that growth has diminished the attention paid to problems associated with other types of state taxes. Legislators have been less willing to deal with a shrinking sales and corporate tax base during times of record budget surpluses. Expanding the tax base, even as part of comprehensive reform, is often perceived as increasing tax burdens. Lawmakers from both political parties would be hard-pressed to accept broadening the base when economic times are good. Solutions to many fiscal problems will be delayed as the personal income tax continues to raise ever-increasing revenue.

Despite the bias on the part of lawmakers to cut rather than raise personal income taxes, the tax has become the dominant source of state revenue. But overreliance may pose a problem for the income tax itself. A slowing economy, the aging work force, decreasing sources of other revenue, and expanding public service needs could result in higher personal income tax rates. Public support could erode quickly if states significantly increase rates. Higher rates also often lead political leaders to grant more and more expansive deductions, exemptions, and credits to various groups. Such tax preferences increase the tax's complexity and often lead to greater compliance and administration burdens.

Perhaps ironically, one key to maintaining a viable personal income tax that will be capable of funding public services may be to strengthen other state taxes. Greater reliance on consumption and corporate income taxes could eliminate the need to raise personal income tax rates and to further complicate the tax system.

NOTES

1. All state tax data are from U.S. Census Bureau (2000).
2. Not surprisingly, New Hampshire and Tennessee came closest to adopting the tax in the past few years. Both states lack significant revenue from severance and tourist taxes.
3. A review of State Tax Notes' comprehensive coverage of gubernatorial campaigns during the 1990s reveals that the personal income tax was the central focus of only one race for governor.
4. Many economists believe that if lifetime income is the measure of wealth, the personal income tax is more proportional than progressive because the young and the elderly tend to earn less (Zodrow 1999). However, since tax liability generally must be paid out of current income, lifetime incidence is a less important measure for most people.

REFERENCES

Bright, Joseph. 1998. *Summary of Pennsylvania Jurisprudence: Taxation.* St. Paul, Minn.: West Group.

Brunori, David. 1998. "State Personal Income Taxes in the 21st Century." In *The Future of State Taxation*, edited by David Brunori (191–206). Washington, D.C.: Urban Institute Press.

———. 1999a. "Interview: FTA's Harley Duncan on the MTC, Cooperation, E-Commerce." *State Tax Notes* (October 8): 1037–1041.

———. 1999b. "Interview: John L. Mikesell on the Present and Future of the Sales Tax." *State Tax Notes* (November 22): 1364–1373.

Bucks, Dan. 1995. "Federal Tax Restructuring: Perils and Possibilities for the States." *State Tax Notes* (August 7): 413–418.

Cline, Robert. 1986. *"Personal Income Tax."* In *Reforming State Tax Systems*, edited by Steven Gold (185–210). Washington, D.C.: National Conference of State Legislatures.

Cole, Richard L., and John Kincaid. 2000. "Public Opinion and American Federalism: Perspectives on Taxes, Spending, and Trust—An ACIR Update." *Publius* 30 (winter/spring): 189–201.

Courtwright, Chris, W. 1998. "Kansas Governor Rejects Proposed Phaseout of Income Tax." *State Tax Notes* (December 27): 1579.

Dearborn, Philip M. 1993. "1993 ACIR 1993 Poll Takes the Public Pulse on Taxes." *State Tax Notes* (October 4): 981–983.

Federation of Tax Administrators (FTA). 1999. "State Tax Collections by State." Http://www.taxadmin.org/fta/rate.

Gold, Steven. 1991. "Interstate Competition and State Personal Income Tax Policies in the 1980s." In *Competition among State and Local Governments*, edited by John Kincaid and Daphne Kenyon (205–213). Washington, D.C.: Urban Institute Press.

Johnson, Nicholas, and Iris Lav. 1997. "Are State Taxes Becoming More Regressive?" *State Tax Notes* (October 6): 893–895.

Lav, Iris, and Steven Gold. 1993. *The States and the Poor*. Washington, D.C.: Center on Budget and Policy Priorities.

Liebschutz, David, S. 1998. "State Taxes and the Family." *State Tax Notes* (March 2): 698–706.

Mackey, Scott. 1996. "State Tax Actions 1996." *State Tax Notes* (November 18): 1459–1489.

Megna, Robert. 1997. "Potential Impact of a National Sales Tax on State Fiscal Policy." *State Tax Notes* (June 2): 1667–1677.

National Conference of State Legislatures (NCSL). 1992. *Principles of a High-Quality State Revenue System*, 2d. ed. Washington, D.C.: NCSL.

———. 1993. *Financing State Government in the 1990s*. Washington, D.C.: NCSL.

———. 2000. *State Budget and Tax Actions*. Washington, D.C.: NCSL.

Sheffrin, Steven. 1996. "Should the Federal Income Tax Be Replaced with a National Sales Tax?" *State Tax Notes* (October 21): 1147–1156.

U.S. Census Bureau. 2000. "Federal, State, and Local Governments: 1998 State Government Finance Data." Http://www.census.gov/govs/www/state98.html.

Zodrow, George. 1999. *State Sales and Income Taxes*. College Station, Tex.: Texas A&M University Press.

7

Corporate
Income Taxes

The corporate tax requires constant vigilance,
maintenance, and repair.

—Richard Pomp (1998)

Forty-six states tax corporate net income, including traditionally anti-income tax jurisdictions such as Tennessee, New Hampshire, and Florida. In 1998, the tax accounted for about $31 billion in tax revenue for the states, according to the U.S. Census Bureau.[1] Only Nevada, Washington, and Wyoming do not impose any taxes on corporate income.[2]

State corporate income and franchise taxes are among the most complicated and controversial components of state revenue systems. The application of the tax to interstate corporate business is one particularly complicated area. Formulary apportionment, distinctions between business and nonbusiness income, and a myriad of planning opportunities test veteran and novice tax practitioners at every filing. Attorneys and accountants struggle with laws designed to raise revenue, spur economic development, and comply with constitutional and federal statutory limitations on state taxing authority.

Controversies naturally arise when states attempt to get their most powerful economic institutions to pay for government services. Corporations have the means to influence tax policy to a greater extent than almost any other interest group. Corporate interests often bring forceful policy arguments—some valid, some less so—for minimizing business and corporate taxes.

Corporate income taxes make up a surprisingly small portion of state revenues. In 1998, corporate income and franchise taxes accounted for only about 6 percent of state tax revenue, and the relative importance of the tax has steadily declined for decades. From its high of about 9.5 percent in 1977, the state corporate income tax dropped to about 6 percent of total state tax revenue in 1998. The corporate income tax's importance is dwarfed by the much larger amount of revenue collected from personal income, consumption, and excise taxes.

Nonetheless, inordinate amounts of resources and intellectual capital are used in administering and complying with state corporate income and franchise taxes. Tax commentators and scholars have noted the difference in administrative and compliance costs for the corporate income tax relative to other levies (Pomp 1998). The reason for this cost/benefit imbalance is that corporations generally have the resources to plan—and when necessary to dispute—tax matters. Specifically, corporations are able to employ highly trained and skilled lawyers, accountants, and economists. Maintaining this expertise also raises corporations' compliance costs.

The private sector's highly trained, well-paid attorneys and accountants also significantly raise the costs of administering the corporate income tax for the states. To meet the companies' intellectual firepower, the states must hire, train, and retain equally qualified tax professionals. Although the state corporate income tax raises very little revenue compared with other levies, it devours a disproportionate amount of planning and litigation resources.

In many cases, the amount of time and resources devoted to the tax outweighs its financial contribution to the states. Even in states with long traditions of progressive taxation, which would seem most likely to rely on the tax, the revenue gained from corporate taxes is minimal. For example, Oregon, historically one of the most progressive states in terms of taxation, has no sales tax and a history of relatively high personal income taxes. Despite this progressive tradition, the state raised only 5.6 percent of its tax revenue from corporate levies in 1998. Oregon raised nearly twice the amount from its lottery operations ($551 million) than it did from its corporate income tax ($279 million).

Indeed, most states collect only a small fraction of their revenue from corporate income taxes. In 1998, on average, the states imposing the tax collected less than 9 percent of their tax revenue from corporate levies. And 18 of these states collected less than 5 percent of their total tax revenue from corporate levies.

The three states most dependent on corporate income taxes are Alaska, New Hampshire, and Delaware; in these states, the tax accounts for 23.2 percent, 23.4 percent, and 10.4 percent of total state tax revenue, respectively.[3] It should be noted, however, that these three states do not impose statewide sales tax. Alaska and New Hampshire also do not tax personal income.

Historical Underpinnings

Although states have imposed taxes on various business activities since the nation's start, today's corporate net income tax can be traced to Wisconsin's Income Tax Law of 1911. The tax proved successful in progressive Wisconsin, and its success quickly led to adoption of the corporate income tax by five other states. By 1930, 17 more states had adopted the tax; by 1940, an additional 17 states had begun taxing corporate income.

The relatively rapid spread of state corporate taxation is attributable to a number of political and economic factors. Progressive and populist political leaders with a skeptical view of corporations controlled many states in the early part of the 20th century. The opportunity to raise revenue from corporations fit naturally with their political philosophies. These same leaders fought successfully to implement progressive personal income taxes at the federal and state levels.

The growth of the corporate tax in the mid-1900s also reflected a developing movement in most states to diversify their tax systems. Throughout the 19th century, state governments financed their operations mainly through excise and some form of property taxes. These financing systems, however, did not raise enough revenue to meet growing public service demands. The early and mid-20th century saw the adoption of personal income taxes as well as sales and use taxes throughout the country. The tax on corporate income was part of the expansion to diversify the overall tax base. These fundamental changes to how states collect revenue have persisted into the start of this century.

Like other levies, the state corporate income tax was developed for a far different economy. The tax was designed at a time when most corporations manufactured tangible personal property. It was also designed to function in an environment in which interstate tax competition was not nearly as intense as it is today. Although that economy no longer dominates, the tax has largely remained the same.[4]

Rationale for the Corporate Income Tax

The state corporate income tax can be justified on a number of grounds. One widely noted rationale is that it compensates for deficiencies in the property tax (Brunori 2000). The property tax does not take into account that businesses require varying degrees of property inputs to produce the same level of profit. Consequently, capital-intensive operations (e.g., manufacturing companies) are taxed more heavily by the property tax than are labor-intensive companies, including knowledge-based enterprises such as high-technology companies. This inequity is compounded by the difficulties in assessing property taxes for intangible property. Instead of relying entirely on taxing business inputs, states, in the interest of greater equity, have included a corporate income tax in their mix of revenue sources (Brunori 2000).

A more common rationale for the corporate income tax is that it protects the much more significant (in terms of revenue) personal income tax. Without a levy on corporate income, taxpayers might have an incentive to shelter personal income in corporate holdings. For example, business owners seeking to avoid personal income tax would incorporate their operations; the corporation itself would then accumulate the dividends or salary that normally would be paid out to the individual. The shareholders could thus escape personal income taxation on these monies until they were paid out as dividends or the company was sold. The federal government, of course, has adopted rules to prevent the accumulation of corporate profits as a means of avoiding personal income tax liability.

This rationale—that the corporate income tax helps protect the personal income tax—makes sense intuitively. However, the increasing number of corporate tax exemptions in recent years undermines its validity. Savvy tax practitioners and state administrators have long recognized that a corporate entity could be used to shelter personal income. The federal government, of course, has adopted rules to prevent the accumulation of corporate profits as a means of avoiding personal income tax liability.[5] As discussed in Chapter 6, personal income tax revenue has grown dramatically in the last decade, a period when corporations increasingly avoided state taxation of income. It is difficult to see how the personal income tax could receive protection from a tax that has proved quite ineffectual in the past quarter-century. Indeed the corporate income tax is badly in need of reform if it is to become a viable source of income for the states.

Of course, an effective corporate income tax system may add to the tremendous success of the personal income tax. But the deficiencies in the state corporate tax system do not generally stem from individuals trying to shelter profits from personal income taxes but rather from corporations' attempts to escape entity-level taxation. Thus, based on the historical record, it is unclear whether the corporate income tax can be justified based on the need to protect the personal income tax.

The most compelling rationale for imposing tax on corporate profits is that such levies reimburse the states for the significant services provided to the business community (Brunori 1999e). Requiring corporations to pay for services provided by the community satisfies the benefits theory of taxation—that is, that tax liabilities are imposed to compensate for the benefits received.

Corporations use public services provided by the state as much as individuals and unincorporated businesses. They benefit from a state's transportation infrastructure—the roads, railways, airports, and harbors used to receive materials and to move products to market. Corporations also benefit from public safety operations, including police, fire, and medical emergency services. In addition, the state judicial system protects their contractual, intellectual property, and other legal rights. Corporations also depend on the state's school system to produce an educated workforce—an especially important role in this highly specialized age of electronic commerce. High-quality school systems also help attract qualified employees.

A corporation's success depends on the adequate provision of these services. In numerous cases, businesses have opposed state tax cuts (or, less frequently, advocated tax increases) to protect public services deemed vital to companies' operations (Brunori 1999b). Many studies have shown that corporations make decisions on where to expand (or relocate) largely based on the availability of adequate public services (Bartik 1991; Lynch 1996).

Opponents of corporate taxes often argue that the economic development and the wealth created by corporations outweigh the benefits that they receive from the state. It is true that corporate enterprises usually result in additional tax revenue for the state in which they operate. The corporation itself, as well as employees of the corporation, pay property and consumption taxes. Employees also pay personal income taxes. But corporate activities can have an even a greater impact on state revenue. When the corporation and its employees spend money, other businesses in the state (e.g., vendors to the corporation and their employees) end up paying income, consumption, and property taxes.

While there are significant advantages to having corporations operate in a particular state, the ultimate beneficiaries of public services provided to corporations are the shareholders. The owners of the corporation receive the profits and enhanced stock value from successful business operations. In today's economy, those shareholders are likely to reside out of state or may themselves be corporations (especially in the case of publicly traded corporations). Only corporate income taxes can be directly linked to the operations of the corporation and are thus paid by the party that ultimately benefits from the public services.

A state's personal income, consumption, and excise taxes are, after all, not necessarily paid by the shareholders of corporations doing business in the state. As noted above, local property taxes represent a benefits tax, but one that falls more heavily on capital-intensive operations. The property tax does not generally reflect the benefits received by companies relying more heavily on intellectual capital than on plant and equipment.

The only way the true beneficiaries of public services provided to corporations can reimburse the state is through the corporate income tax. No other levy accurately places the burden of paying for government on those who actually receive the benefits.

Finally, an important justification for the corporate tax is that it eases—to some extent—the regressivity of state tax systems. The corporate income tax generally has a progressive effect on the state's overall public finance system. While a broader segment of the population owns corporate stock than ever before, most of the corporate wealth remains in the hands of the wealthy. Along with the personal income tax, the corporate income tax offsets the regressive effects of the sales and use taxes as well as the excise taxes imposed by many states.

Policy Issues: The Failure of the State Corporate Income Tax

The state corporate income tax presents numerous issues for state and national policymakers. Although many of these issues have existed since the inception of the tax, others are the result of modern economic, technological, and political developments.

The state corporate income tax has not been a particularly reliable or stable source of income for state governments. The percentage of total state tax revenue collected from levies on corporate income has declined steadily for more than two decades. Many commentators expect that decline to continue (Brunori 1999c; Brunori 1999d).

In 32 states, the share of corporate income tax relative to total state tax revenue fell between 1995 and 1998 (Dubin 1999). As noted above, only two states, New Hampshire and Alaska, still collect more than 20 percent of their total tax revenue from the corporate taxes. But their unusually heavy reliance on the tax reflects the decision not to tax personal income and sales more than any philosophical agreement with corporate taxation.

More important, in every year since 1959 the corporate tax base has failed to keep pace with company profits (either worldwide or domestic) (Dubin 1999). In other words, in relative terms, state governments are collecting less in corporate income taxes while corporations are earning more. Some of the major reasons for the decline in the state corporate income tax are discussed below.

Tax Incentives and the Abandonment of Uniformity

One important factor in the steady erosion of the state corporate tax base is the pervasive use of targeted tax incentives. Each year, literally hundreds of tax breaks are granted to corporations to encourage economic development. In addition to sales and property tax incentives, states provide significant corporate income tax incentives as part of their effort to retain or attract businesses. Corporate income tax incentives generally include tax credits for investment, job creation, and worker training as well as expanded deductions for accelerated depreciation. These tax expenditures cost state governments (and state taxpayers) billions of dollars in forgone revenue. They are offered every year by state taxing corporate income (Brunori 1997; Pomp 1998). Despite their ineffectiveness, tax incentives have proliferated in the past quarter-century.

The most noteworthy example is the "Mercedes-Benz" law. Enacted in Alabama, the law was meant to entice the German automaker to remain in the state. Under the law, companies that invest at least $5 million and employ at least 50 people in the state are allowed to issue tax-exempt bonds to finance their operations. The companies can then claim corporate income tax credits for the amount spent servicing the debt on the bonds. The law provided Mercedes-Benz with more than $250 million in tax breaks, the majority of which reduced the company's corporate income tax liability. Alabama raises less than 4 percent of its total tax revenue from corporate taxes, a below-average percentage that is almost certainly related to the Mercedes-Benz law.

Tax incentives limit a state's ability to tax corporations on their net profits. But the problem is that such incentives are rarely limited to a small number of companies. The willingness of states to offer tax incentives creates an atmosphere that encourages companies to seek the same type of tax preferences offered to other companies. Corporations count on the states' propensity to offer tax incentives, and many corporate investment decisions are coupled with a request for incentives. Often these requests are made after the company has already made its investment and location decisions (Brunori 1997). Once states begin offering tax incentives to a lucky few corporations, it is very difficult not to offer similar incentives to many companies. The result is a declining corporate tax base.[6]

States have also attempted to use their corporate tax laws to foster economic development with another, less publicly known, method. To promote interstate commerce, many states have modified the formulas they use to calculate corporate income tax. The use of different apportionment formulas among the states essentially disregards the notion that an effective corporate income tax system requires uniformity across state lines. When the corporate income tax was first implemented, many corporations manufactured, sold, and had headquarters in one or a few states. There were few problems in determining which states had jurisdiction to tax corporate profits. In the modern economy, however, it is difficult to find many corporations that do not conduct multistate business.

For the state corporate income tax to work effectively for interstate business, uniformity is essential (Brunori 2000; Pomp 1998). The principle of uniformity requires that all states imposing corporate income taxes use the same (or very similar) rules for determining how corporations are taxed and which states have authority to tax corporate income. The use of uniform laws facilitates the accurate determination of tax liability among multistate taxpayers, including the equitable apportionment of tax bases. Uniformity also reduces the compliance costs (return preparation and filing) for taxpayers. Perhaps most important, if every state used the three-factor formula, corporations would neither be taxed twice on the same income nor be able to avoid taxation on 100 percent of their income. Moreover, corporations would not have the incentive or the ability to base business decisions on corporate tax consequences.

For state governments, uniformity decreases the costs of administration. Uniformity also ensures that corporations conducting business in states that impose corporate income taxes will pay their fair share of taxes. If all states adopted the same or very similar rules, corporations would be unable to create "nowhere income" that is not subject to tax.

To achieve a measure of uniformity, in the past most states relied on the evenly weighted three-factor apportionment formula adopted by the 1957 Uniform Division of Income for Tax Purposes Act. This three-factor formula apportions taxable income according to the relative amount of sales, property, and payroll a corporation has in a particular state. These three factors approximate the value added to the corporation's business in the various states. States began to adopt different apportionment formulas as a way to foster economic development. Twenty-five states imposing the corporate income tax now double-weight the sales factor. Iowa, Nebraska, Texas, and Illinois[7] use a single-sales factor to determine corporate tax liability. Using a double-weighted or single-sales factor usually results in lower tax burdens for corporations that have substantial operations within a state (as measured by payroll and property) but sell most of their goods and services out of state. In effect, double-weighting the sales factor benefits corporations with significant property and payroll in the state. Accordingly, many politically powerful corporations have lobbied for a formula that double-weights sales (Pomp 1998).

Not all corporations benefit from using an apportionment formula with a double- or single-sales factor, since this method increases the tax burdens on corporations that sell a significant share of their products in a particular state but do not maintain sizable operations in that state. State policymakers often accept this imbalance, however, to meet the larger goal of attracting investment. They reason that corporations are unlikely to stop selling their products and making profits in a state merely because their tax burdens are somewhat higher than those of businesses located within the state (Pomp 1998).

Although lawmakers believe that a double- or single-sales factor will encourage companies to expand their presence in the state, there is no real evidence that deviating from the traditional three-factor formula promotes economic development (Pomp 1987). The ultimate effect is to shrink the in-state corporate tax base. The move to the double- or single-sales factor has resulted in an annual loss of $500 million (Pomp 1998). This loss is no small amount for a tax that raises just over $30 billion in revenue per year.[8]

The Effects of Aggressive Planning

Another important shortcoming of the corporate income tax system is that most states fail to combine the apportionment factors of related entities when calculating tax liabilities. In these "separate-entity states," the property, sales, and payroll of related corporations engaged in the same business are not taken into account. Thus, each corporation calculates its corporate tax liability without regard to related-party transactions.

As an alternative to the separate-entity policy, states could require related corporations engaged in the same "unitary business" to calculate their apportionment formula as if they were operating one business. This requirement would eliminate intercompany transactions and combine the sales, property, and payroll of the related parties.

As noted by Pomp (1998), failure to require combined reporting results in a direct link between corporate income tax liability and the legal structure of the corporate group. The choice to operate as a subsidiary or division will often create dramatically different tax consequences even though there is no real economic difference between the two arrangements. Corporate tax planners routinely take advantage of the opportunity to avoid or lessen corporate tax liability by simply incorporating a division or liquidating a subsidiary. Often, this action has no other business or economic reason; it is taken solely to avoid the tax.

States' failure to require combined reporting also allows related corporations to shift profits from states with relatively high tax burdens to states with lower or no corporate tax burdens. When related corporations conduct a single unitary business, they have the opportunity to manipulate prices. For example, a corporation in state A (with a high effective tax rate) might sell products to a related corporation in state B (with a low effective tax rate) at prices well below market. If the related corporation's operations are not combined with the original seller's operations for tax purposes, the companies will have shifted the profits from state A to state B and reduced the overall tax burden. Policing such transfer pricing is an expensive and difficult endeavor for the states (Egr 1996).

The failure to require combined reporting also gives companies incentive to establish holding companies in states that do not impose corporate income tax on these entities, such as Delaware and Nevada. The holding company is established to do little more than collect royalties and interest from its related companies. The royalties and interest are usually deducted from the related party's taxable income, but the holding company typically is not taxed on the receipts.

Pomp (1998) proposes another reason for states' inability to collect the amount of corporate tax revenue that the potential tax base suggests is possible. He theorizes that aggressive planning on the part of the corporate tax bar effectively allows corporations to escape taxation.[9]

Like federal tax practices, state corporate tax firms attract the top accountants and lawyers in the field. The corporate planning and litigation resources in this area continually challenge state revenue departments. Corporations and their representatives in large law firms and the Big 5 accounting firms have the resources (and the incentive) to develop sophisticated planning devices to legally minimize state tax liability. Developments in the past decade illustrate that they have successfully used those resources to reduce corporate tax burdens.

For example, only "business income" (income from the same business operations) is subject to apportionment among the states in which the corporation has sales, payroll, and property. Non-business income (interest, dividends, and income unrelated to the operations of the taxable business) is not subject to apportionment but is allocated to the state that is considered the source of the income. Corporate planners have been particularly adept at converting what would normally be considered business income to non-business income allocated to a low- or no-income tax state (Pomp 1998).

Pass-Through Entities: The Rise of LLCs/LLPs

Part of the decline of the state corporate income tax has been caused by the dramatic growth in the use of pass-through entities to carry out multistate business. Limited liability companies (LLCs) and limited liability partnerships (LLPs) have increasingly become the entity of choice for many businesses that traditionally would have opted for C corporate status (Lee 2000). Changes in federal law in 1995 made electing LLC and LLP entity status much easier for the purposes of federal taxation. Under most states' laws, LLCs and LLPs that are treated as partnerships for federal tax purposes are treated the same way for state tax purposes (Ely and Grissom 2000).

Businesses operating as LLCs and LLPs are not taxed at the entity (i.e., at the corporate or partnership) level. Rather, the taxable income passes through to the shareholders and partners. This arrangement avoids one of the oldest complaints about the corporate tax at both the federal and state levels: double taxation of profits. Partnerships and federal S corporations have always avoided this pitfall. But the advantage of LLCs and LLPs is that the shareholders and partners enjoy virtually the same protections against personal liability as do traditional C corporations.

The potential problem for state revenue departments is that more and more businesses will choose to operate as LLCs and LLPs, further shrinking the corporate tax base. While a serious concern, the growth of the use of pass-through entities may not continue at the same pace (Lee 2000). LLCs and LLPs do not offer easy access to capital, and they offer no opportunity to trade stock publicly. In an economy driven by the need for capital at a moment's notice, many businesses will continue to choose to operate as traditional C corporations.

Outlook for the State Corporate Income Tax: Should It Be Imposed?

Given the relatively small amount of revenue generated by the corporate income tax, as well as the high costs of compliance and administration, a relevant question is whether the states should impose the tax at all. Of course, if the percentage of corporate income tax revenue continues to fall, legislative abolition may not even be necessary.

Many experts believe that the corporate income tax is neither an efficient nor an effective method for raising state revenue. James Peters, a nationally known practitioner who has served with the California Franchise Tax Board, concludes that "there is little theoretical support for the tax" (Peters 1995, 1404). Economist Peggy Musgrave notes that the "corporate income tax at the state level has run counter to the recommendations of most economists who have traditionally seen the tax as a particularly inefficient and inequitable instrument, singularly unsuited for use at the state level" (Musgrave 1984, 51). As far back as 1981, former Deputy Assistant Secretary of the Treasury for Tax Analysis Charles

McLure asserted that state corporate income taxes have manifest disadvantages that disqualify them for use by states (McLure 1981, 51). More recently, McLure notes, "The primary reasons for a state corporate income tax are cosmetic and political; it is simply not politically acceptable for individuals to pay income taxes if corporations do not" (Brunori 1999c, 1227).

Despite these notable detractors, there is no widespread public or political support for eliminating the tax. Support may be lacking because the revenue and burdens generated by the tax are too inconsequential to give rise to serious dissatisfaction. But the reason may be that, despite the problems discussed above, political leaders and the public sincerely agree with the rationale for imposing a tax on corporate profits. Without the tax, even the pretense that corporations (or rather their shareholders) pay for the government services they receive would disappear.

With no serious opposition to the tax on the horizon, the state corporate income tax will no doubt continue to exist. Unless states strengthen the tax considerably, however, it will remain a minor source of revenue.

Strengthening the Corporate Income Tax

How can states rescue the state corporate income tax from near irrelevancy and make it a more significant source of income? Three policy changes could strengthen the tax. First, the states could end the wasteful practice of offering tax incentives to corporations. Tax incentives have essentially gutted the corporate tax base, yet states have been unwilling and unable to stop offering incentives to corporations.

For years, there has been talk of enacting legislation under the Commerce Clause to prohibit the use of targeted tax incentives. But neither Congress nor the states have shown much interest in such legislation. The states appear much more concerned (perhaps justifiably) about losing autonomy over their finances than about a shrinking corporate tax base. Thus, federal legislation to prohibit targeted tax incentives is unlikely.

Given the political constraints, probably the best way to reduce the use of corporate tax incentives is to better educate lawmakers about the incentives' disadvantages. Various groups have made serious efforts to inform legislators and governors that tax incentives exemplify unsound tax policy. Organizations such as the Corporation for Enterprise Development, the Center on Budget and Policy Priorities, and Good Jobs First have conducted studies illustrating the problems created by incentives. In addition, the mainstream media and trade publications such as *State Tax Notes* have increasingly highlighted the political and policy issues surrounding the use of targeted tax incentives. Public and political leaders who know why incentives are ineffective are more likely to question their use.

Another possible solution for strengthening the corporate income tax is for states to require unitary-based combined reporting for all related corporations. Under this requirement, all related corporations would apportion their respective state tax returns as a single business. The combined reporting requirement would severely limit the ability of corporations to use tax planning techniques to avoid state corporate tax liability. It would also add billions of dollars to state revenue (Pomp 1998). Corporations, however, are generally opposed to combined reporting requirements and would likely challenge any attempt to mandate them.

The possibility of strengthening the corporate income tax depends on all the states working toward this goal. Reliance on different tax bases and the use of different apportionment formulas create opportunities for corporate tax avoidance in the states (Pomp 1998). The most effective way to strengthen the tax base is for the states to adhere to the principles set forth in the Multistate Tax Compact, which emphasizes uniformity among and cooperation between the states. Moreover, the states imposing corporate income tax should work with the Multistate Tax Commission to develop uniform rules that will benefit the states as well as corporate taxpayers.

Uniformity in the tax base and apportionment formulas would reduce compliance and administrative costs. It would also remove the incentive to develop expensive tactics that take advantage of the myriad rules and regulations across states. Uniformity would ease the problems of double taxation and, most important, limit the opportunity of corporations to avoid their obligations of paying for the government services they receive.

It is up to the state political leaders whether to pursue these courses of action. But to save the corporate income tax from irrelevancy, policymakers must find ways to strengthen and enforce the tax.

NOTES

1. All data on corporate income tax revenue are for 1998 and are from the U.S. Census Bureau (2000). The relatively small amount of corporate income tax revenue reflects an overall reduction in state taxation of business income. One study found that 41 percent of all taxes paid by business were levies on real property (Swenson 1997).
2. Washington's business and occupation tax is viewed as a business activity tax on gross income.
3. Michigan enacted the single-business tax on corporations in 1976. The legislature enacted a long-term phaseout of the tax (23 years) in 1999 (Brunori 1999a). Michigan had collected more than 10 percent of its tax revenue from the single-business tax, but that percentage will certainly decline as the phaseout progresses.
4. Pomp (1998) points out that the states have been successful at modifying some aspects of how they tax corporate income to reflect the changing economy.
5. See 26 U.S.C. sec. 531.
6. Nebraska, for example, enacted a law at the insistence of ConAgra, Inc., which threatened to move its corporate headquarters from Omaha. To appease the company, the state offered additional investment tax credits. Initially, the law was thought to benefit a handful of companies in addition to ConAgra. Because of the structure of the program, however, more than 200 companies had applied and/or qualified for the tax credits within six years of its enactment (Wesely 1993).
7. Massachusetts and Connecticut allow single-factor apportionment for certain industries.
8. Deviating from the traditional apportionment formula also allows corporations to take advantage of Public Law 86-272, which prohibits a state from imposing income taxes on a corporation that is only selling products in the state (Pomp 1998, 58).
9. Not all state public finance experts would agree that the states are outmatched by the private bar (Brunori 2000).

REFERENCES

Bartik, Timothy. 1991. *Who Benefits from State and Local Economic Development Policies?* Kalamazoo, Mich.: W.E. Upjohn Institute for Employment Research.
Brunori, David. 1997. "Principles of Tax Policy and Targeted Tax Incentives." *State and Local Government Review* 29 (1, winter): 50–61.
———. 1999a. "The Long Fadeout of Michigan's SBT." *State Tax Notes* (October 11): 965–967.
———. 1999b. "Business Makes Its Case—For Higher Taxes." *State Tax Notes* (September 13): 683–686.
———. 1999c. "Interview: Charles McLure on Sales Tax, E-Commerce, and the Pros and Cons of a VAT." *State Tax Notes* (November 8): 1225–1230.
———. 1999d. "Interview: FTA's Harley Duncan on the MTC, Cooperation, E-Commerce." *State Tax Notes* (October 18): 1037–1041.

———. 1999e. "Interview: CBPP's Iris Lav on Fairness, Progressivity, and the Net." *State Tax Notes* (October 25): 1103–1108.

———. 2000. "Interview with Dan Bucks of the Multistate Tax Commission." *State Tax Notes* (July 31): 303–309.

Dubin, Elliot. 1999. Paper presented to the Multistate Tax Commission Annual Conference, Traverse City, Mich., July 29.

Egr, Mary Jane. 1996. "State Section 482–Type Authority." *State Tax Notes* (November 25): 1545–1554.

Ely, Bruce, and Christopher Grissom. 2000. "LLC and LLP Scorecard: An Update." *State Tax Notes* (July 24): 235–243.

Lee, John William, III. 2000. "Choice of Small Business Tax Entity: Fact and Fiction." *State Tax Notes* (May 8): 1605–1620.

Lynch, Robert. 1996. "Do State and Local Tax Incentives Work?" Washington, D.C.: Economic Policy Institute.

McLure, Charles. 1981. "Toward Uniformity in Interstate Taxation." *Tax Notes* (July 13): 51.

Musgrave, Peggy. 1984. *Principles for Dividing the State Corporate Tax Base*. In *The State Corporation Income Tax*, edited by Charles McLure (51). Palo Alto, Calif.: Hoover Institution Press.

Peters, James H. 1995. "The State Corporation Income Tax in the 21st Century." *State Tax Notes* (April 3): 1400–1404.

Pomp, Richard. 1998. "The Future of the State Corporate Income Tax: Reflections (and Confessions) of a State Tax Lawyer." In *The Future of State Taxation*, edited by David Brunori (49–72). Washington, D.C.: Urban Institute Press.

———. 1987. "Reforming a Corporate Income Tax." *Albany Law Review* 51: 393–409.

Swenson, Charles W. 1997. "Does Your State Overtax Business Income?" *State Tax Notes* (November 3): 1129–1135.

U.S. Census Bureau. 2000. "Federal, State, and Local Governments: 1998 State Government Finance Data." Http://www.census.gov/govs/www/state98.html.

Wesely, Don. 1993. "Myths and Realities of Economic Development Incentives: Who's Giving Away the Store? Revisited." *State Tax Notes* (September 20): 645.

8

Other State Taxes

We have how many taxes? Makes you want to vote Republican.

—Democratic legislator, when told that his
state has more than 30 distinct taxes.

State governments impose a variety of taxes other than personal income, corporate income, and sales taxes. Altogether, the states administer literally hundreds of different types of taxes.[1] The most important categories include excise, severance, wealth transfer (estate, gift, and inheritance), and property taxes. Together, these four types of taxes account for more than 26 percent of total state tax revenue and 11 percent of total state revenue. In 1998, according to the U.S. Census Bureau, states raised more than $126 billion from these taxes, with some states drawing more than half their total tax revenue from these levies alone.[2]

Out of the $126 billion raised in "other taxes" in 1998, $71.3 billion, or 15 percent, came from the various types of state excise taxes. As this figure demonstrates, the excise tax remains an important revenue source for the states, accounting for about 6 percent of total state revenue. Wealth transfer taxes, severance taxes, property taxes, and the other taxes levied by state governments, however, mostly have a minimal impact on state budgets. In fact, all other taxes combined account for barely 10 percent of total tax revenue for the states. In most cases, each of these taxes accounts for less than 1 percent of total state tax revenue.

Still, excises and the other types of taxes pose serious policy issues for state lawmakers and administrators. Despite the relatively low yield, many of the taxes are unduly complicated and require an inordinate amount of resources to meet compliance and administrative requirements. Some of these taxes present equity issues because their burdens fall most heavily on those least able to pay. And some are perceived to place a state at a competitive disadvantage. Nearly all have been the subject of heated political debate at one time or another. Many of these taxes could be eliminated, because the amount of revenue they generate does not justify the problems presented or the compliance costs of their imposition. Indeed, in the many tax reform studies conducted in the various states, a recurring theme has been to reduce the number of different taxes (e.g., West Virginia Governor's Commission on Fair Taxation [1996] and Ebel and McGuire [1986]).

Excise Taxes

Excises, also called "special" or "selective" sales taxes, encompass many types of levies.[3] States tax alcohol, fuel, tobacco, hotel rooms, car rentals, and many other products and services. Within these broad categories of goods, many types of products are subject to excise levies. For example, all states tax alcohol products, but they impose different tax rates on beer, wine, and liquor, respectively (Federation of Tax Administrators 1999). In addition, all states tax tobacco products, but many impose separate levies on cigarettes, pipe tobacco, chewing tobacco, and cigars. Similarly, every state taxes fuel products, but natural gas, diesel, gasoline, and other petroleum products are often subject to different tax rates and administrative rules.

Excise taxes were the primary source of state revenue before the 20th century. Today, however, excise taxes account for a much smaller part of state tax revenue. The three most widely recognized excise taxes—alcohol ($3 billion), fuel ($28 billion), and tobacco ($7 billion)—together account for approximately $38 billion of state tax revenue. Two additional sources of significant excise revenue are insurance premium taxes (about $9.1 billion) and excise taxes on public utility sales (about $8.7 billion).

Most individual products that are subject to excise taxes provide a relatively small percentage of state revenue, with specific products subject to excise tax typically providing less than 1 percent of total state tax revenue.

Administration of Excise Taxes

Unlike general sales and use taxes, which are imposed on the cost of a product, excise taxes are typically tallied on a per unit basis. For example, the state excise tax on gasoline is imposed on a cents per gallon basis in every state but one; cigarette taxes are imposed on each pack of cigarettes; and taxes on alcohol are imposed by the gallon (or liter, pint, etc.).

Moreover, unlike sales and use taxes, excises generally apply to the first sale of the product within a state. For automobile fuel, the tax is collected at the distributor level or, less frequently, at the refinery level.[4] For tobacco products, the tax is usually collected from the wholesaler. Alcohol taxes are assessed at the distributor level.

Of course, the tax almost always gets passed along to the final purchaser. However, unlike the general sales tax, the excise tax is not stated anywhere for the consumer. Thus, consumers may know that excise taxes exist, but they are usually unaware of the specific tax burdens associated with a particular purchase. In this regard, excise taxes are less transparent than is advocated by the principles of sound tax policy.

Because excise taxes are paid by vendors directly to the government (typically on a monthly or quarterly basis), they have presented few administrative or compliance problems for taxpayers or states. Unlike the tax policy often applied to sales and use taxes, however, most state governments do not do not allow the vendor to retain a small portion of the excise tax to offset the administrative costs of compliance.

Failure to pay the tax can result in significant civil and criminal penalties. Enforcement laws vary from state to state, but excise tax penalties provide a powerful incentive for compliance. To assist the enforcement and administration of excise taxes, states often mark products once the tax has been paid; for example, cigarette stamps denote tobacco taxes paid. Selling products without these identifying marks is usually illegal.

The federal government imposes excises on most of the same products as states. This makes tax evasion less likely, because a vendor would have to deceive two government entities to successfully evade the tax. Excise taxes on alcohol and petroleum products are also very difficult to evade because they are often sold from fixed, licensed establishments.

For excises on tobacco, however, the states must contend with problems of evasion. High tobacco taxes in some states give vendors an incentive to purchase cigarettes from low-tax states. The relative ease of transporting cigarettes across state lines make excise taxes on tobacco products easier to avoid than excises on other products, such as fuel. In recent years, vendors have increasingly turned to the Internet to avoid state tobacco taxes. Many states, in turn, have restricted remote sales of cigarettes and other tobacco products or taken steps to collect the tax from these vendors (Streitfeld 2000).

Rationale for the Tax

Excise taxes serve both revenue and nonrevenue purposes. Because they are imposed for social policy reasons unrelated to paying for public services, excise taxes generally violate one of the fundamental principles of sound tax policy: that taxes be used predominantly to raise revenue to pay for government services.

Tobacco and alcohol taxes are imposed to deter socially undesirable activities and are generally supported by the public. Support for tobacco taxes grew particularly strong in the 1990s, after legal action revealed that the tobacco industry had known of the health risks associated with smoking for some time. The public widely believes that raising cigarette prices through excise taxes will lead some smokers to quit and will deter nonsmokers—especially the young—from starting the habit. This perceived social benefit explains why tobacco taxes have not met significant political resistance. Alcoholism, underage drinking, and the tragedies of drunk-driving accidents have led to widespread public support for taxes on beer, wine, and liquor. Like tobacco taxes, levies on alcohol consumption do not generate much political controversy or opposition.

Besides having deterrence value, excise taxes on tobacco and alcohol are often justified as a way to compensate the states for the substantial costs associated with the products' consumption. Tobacco and alcohol use result in significant government outlays for medical care, education programs, and public safety. By directly taxing the consumers, the state can recoup some of the costs incurred by consumers' reliance on these services. Policymakers view excise taxes as similar to user fees because the burdens fall on the individuals most likely to rely on the government services in question.

Deterring the consumption of harmful products is not the only rationale for excise taxes. Some excises are targeted to fund specific services related to the products and services being taxed. For example, gasoline tax revenue is often specifically earmarked for highway and road expenditures. In this way, the excise tax again is similar to a user fee: Those who buy gasoline for their automobiles and trucks contribute to the upkeep and repair of the roads.

The drawback to this argument is that transportation systems serve the entire public, rather than just drivers using state roads. Everyone who purchases products delivered to stores via the state highways or who relies on services performed by people who travel those roads benefits from a state's road system. Thus, not everyone who benefits from the state highway systems shares in the costs of maintaining those systems, and the costs are unevenly distributed.

Political leaders also cite nonrevenue reasons for imposing fuel taxes. Gasoline taxes are meant to promote fuel conservation and to limit air pollution. But most of the nonrevenue reasons for imposing fuel excise taxes are invoked by federal legislators rather than by state legislators. Lawmakers do not generally use environmental concerns to justify gasoline taxes in the states.

Policy Issues Associated with Excise Taxes

The use of excise taxes presents several important policy issues for legislators, including the government's reliance on "sin taxes" and problems with the fairness and reliability of excise taxes.

RELIANCE ON SIN TAXES TO FUND GOVERNMENT. One of the principles of sound tax policy is that a tax should be used primarily to raise revenue. Taxes used to encourage or discourage individual behavior do not adhere to that principle. Many excise taxes are designed specifically to influence behavior. The rationale for excises on tobacco and alcohol, for example, has also been to deter or limit the use of these products. Excise taxes violate the principle that tax laws should not be used for reasons other than raising revenue to pay for government services. Nonetheless, supporters of excise taxes argue that the effects of these products justify their existence. Besides, they might argue, few policy alternatives are as effective as excise taxes in deterring overuse.[5] Few serious political arguments based on the principle of market neutrality have been made against tobacco and alcohol taxes.

Some excise taxes have the unintended consequence of becoming an important part of the state's budget. Thus, the state finds itself relying to some extent on the purchase of these harmful products. This reliance creates a difficult situation: The state may be trying to deter use by citizens while also protecting its revenue source, placing a state in the position of taxing a product because it is harmful, but trying not to tax it too much because the tax raises substantial revenue.

While tobacco and alcohol taxes do not make up a large percentage of state tax revenue, they still raised more than $10 billion a year in 1998. That amount of revenue makes ending the reliance on sin taxes (even while developing alternative policies for limiting tobacco and alcohol use) difficult (Brunori 1999).

RELIABILITY. Excise taxes do not necessarily keep pace with price levels at a given tax rate. As noted, excise taxes are generally imposed on a per unit (as opposed to ad valorem) basis. As inflation occurs, the price of the underlying product increases, but the related tax revenue does not. This helps explain why the excise tax revenue has continued to fall as a percentage of total state taxes.[6] This phenomenon is a problem in the case of motor-fuel tax revenues earmarked to pay for road and highway maintenance; unlike the tax, the costs of these services increase with inflation. Tobacco tax revenues allocated to health programs suffer the same problem.

FAIRNESS. One of the biggest problems with most state excises is that they are regressive. Poorer citizens pay a far greater percentage of their income in excise taxes than do wealthier taxpayers. Opponents of excise taxes believe that the social problems associated with many of the products subject to these taxes should be addressed through nontax means rather than through a tax that disproportionately burdens the poor.

Some studies have attributed the regressivity of sin taxes to higher use of tobacco and alcohol among low-income individuals than among the wealthy. But of even greater concern is the regressivity of fuel taxes. The single largest percentage of excise tax revenue comes from taxing fuel; motor fuel taxes raised $28.3 billion in 1998—nearly three times as much as taxes on alcohol and tobacco. Fuel taxes are recognized as one of the most regressive types of levies imposed by state governments (Chernick and Reschovsky 2000).

Unfortunately, policymakers arguing against excise taxes often find themselves in the unenviable position of agreeing with the tobacco, liquor, and petroleum industries, which strongly oppose excises intended to reduce consumption of the products that they sell. Political leaders are often wary of taking such a position.

Outlook for Excise Taxes

Excise taxes are a limited revenue option for states. First, there is little opportunity to broaden the base; the few product categories that can accommodate an excise tax are already taxed by many states. Second, at some point, increasing existing excise tax burdens either severely deters use of a product or encourages widespread evasion. Thus, excise tax revenue will likely continue to decline in importance. Moreover, as prices for products subject to excises have increased, calls for reducing excises have also risen. For example, rapidly rising fuel prices in the early 2000s have given rise to suspensions or reductions in gasoline excise taxes in many states (Brunori 2000a). Existing excise tax revenue will likely remain stagnant. The states are unlikely to find ways to either broaden the base or increase rates enough to make the excise tax a more substantial part of state budgets.

Severance Taxes

Severance taxes have been levied since the mid-19th century, when Michigan began imposing a tax on the privilege of mining copper. Severance taxes are levied on nonrenewable natural resources extracted from lands and waters. The tax is typically imposed on mining coal and other minerals, cutting timber, harvesting fish, and extracting oil and natural gas.

Nationwide, the tax is not a significant source of revenue. In 1998, severance taxes raised just over $3 billion and accounted for much less than 1 percent of total state tax revenue. Seventeen states do not collect any severance tax revenue.

In a number of states rich in natural resources, however, severance taxes are an important source of revenue. Alaska, Kentucky, Louisiana, Montana, New Mexico, Oklahoma, North Dakota, Texas, Washington, West Virginia, and Wyoming all rely heavily on severance taxes to fund public services. Each of these states raises more than 5 percent of its total tax revenue from severance taxes. Alaska is the most dependent on severance tax revenue, raising nearly 60 percent of its total state tax revenue from this source.

Severance taxes allow these states to reduce, or in many cases eliminate, other taxes. For example, Alaska, South Dakota, Texas, Washington, and Wyoming do not impose personal income tax. Alaska and Montana do not impose statewide sales taxes.

Virtually all severance tax burdens can be exported to out-of-state residents and businesses. The tax primarily falls on the owners of the property (rather than on broad segments of society) and can easily be passed on as part of the sales price of the minerals or other natural resources. As noted in chapter 4, political leaders have a bias in favor of exporting tax burdens, so severance taxes are generally an attractive policy option.

Severance taxes are imposed both for the substantial revenue they raise (in the states noted above) and to reimburse the state for the loss of its natural resources. Many types of natural resources (e.g., coal) are depletable; once extracted, they cannot be replaced. Severance taxes are a way to compensate the state for that permanent loss. For that reason, severance tax revenue is often placed in a trust or other long-term fund designed to produce revenue when the natural resources are no longer available to raise revenue for the states. Most states also designate some portion of severance tax revenue to reclamation and other environmental programs.

Except in a few states, severance taxes will remain a relatively inconsequential part of revenue systems because prices are volatile and natural resources are limited. Severance taxes are imposed on a per unit basis (e.g., per ton of coal), on an ad valorem basis (on the value of the natural resources extracted), or on a combination of the two. Severance tax revenue is tied explicitly to the market for natural resources. For example, if the price of coal falls, severance tax revenue will decline both because the value of the coal has fallen and because less coal is mined. The volatility of revenues raised by severance taxes is exemplified by the tax's sharp decline from 1998 to 1999; during that short time, severance tax revenue fell from about $4.1 billion to about $3.1 billion, an astonishing 25 percent.

Moreover, the ability to extract natural resources is limited. In many states, environmental protection efforts limit production. For these reasons, severance tax revenue will probably decline in importance.

State Property Taxes

Property taxes have always been the primary source of revenue for local governments.[7] State governments also impose taxes on the value of property. Until the 1930s and the onset of the Great Depression, property taxes accounted for nearly half of total state tax revenue. In 1998, state property taxes accounted for only 2.2 percent of total state tax revenue. The amount of revenue raised from property taxes is small, given that the amount includes state taxes on personal property, intangible property, business property, and real property.

Still, property taxes raised more than $10 billion in state revenue in 1998. And three states (Montana, Washington, and Wyoming) raised more than 10 percent of their revenue from statewide property taxes. These states' heavier reliance on the property tax is attributable in part to their decision not to impose sales or income taxes.

Types of State Property Taxes

REAL PROPERTY. Eight states levy broad-based taxes on all property subject to local property taxes. In general, these taxes are usually imposed on real property. The tax on real property has been one of the most stable and reliable sources of revenue for local and state governments. Real property values rise over time; this increased valuation translates into increased revenue. Significantly, the revenue increases do not carry the political risks of raising tax rates. Moreover, property taxes are politically palatable because in most cases they can be deducted from federal taxable income.

The compliance and administration costs of property taxation are low compared with those for other types of levies. State governments rely on local jurisdictions to carry out much of the administration of the tax. Local governments generally assess and collect the state portion of the property tax and remit payment to the state government. Real property tax administration is cost-effective because the property cannot be moved. And property taxes are generally difficult to evade.

For taxpayers, too, the costs of compliance are relatively low. The government assesses and bills the property owner. The taxpayer merely pays the tax on the assessed value. Typically, no forms or returns are filed and records do not need to be kept (except for federal tax-deduction purposes).

For several reasons, however, property taxes imposed both by state and local governments have been unpopular. The tax unduly burdens fixed-income owners of property, especially when property values are increasing rapidly. In addition, the tax has often been unfairly administered; in the past, many similar properties in the same geographic area have had vastly different assessment values. Significant reforms over the past quarter-century, however, have corrected many of the problems associated with real property taxation. Rate and assessment limitations and homestead exemptions protect low-income and elderly property owners. Sophisticated assessment methods have greatly improved the accuracy and fairness of administration.

State governments are limited in their ability to rely on property taxes because these taxes have traditionally been a source of revenue for local governments. Like sales and income taxes for state governments, the property tax gives local governments substantial autonomy and flexibility over their budgets.

TANGIBLE PERSONAL PROPERTY TAXES. Many states continue to tax the value of tangible personal property.[8] But the tax has always been limited to a small number of items. Most types of tangible personal property cannot be taxed effectively because they can be easily moved or hidden. Moreover, the valuation process is administratively difficult.

States have generally limited the tax on tangible personal property to motor vehicles such as cars, boats, and airplanes, because vehicles are registered with the state. At least 30 states impose some type of tax on the value of motor vehicles or allow local governments to do so (Mackey and Rafool 1998).

Property taxes on motor vehicles have proved to be among the most unpopular of all levies. The criticism of the tax has focused on the relatively high burdens on consumers (especially for new-car owners), recurring payments on a depreciating asset, and the negative effect on new-car purchases (a complaint among car dealerships). Serious movements to repeal or reduce the tax have sprung up in many states since Virginia began the repeal of its car tax in 1997. While efforts to repeal the tax have abated, the tax remains highly unpopular.

TAXATION OF BUSINESS PROPERTY. Businesses also pay property taxes on tangible personal property, including motor vehicles. The bulk of business property taxes, however, falls on inventory, machinery, and equipment. In recent years, the trend has been to eliminate or dramatically reduce taxes on businesses' tangible personal property. Businesses that own considerable machinery and equipment have increasingly and successfully argued that these levies put them at a competitive disadvantage. Similarly, businesses that hold substantial inventory argue that they are penalized, especially during economic downturns.

Outlook for the Property Tax

The property tax is an inconsequential part of the state public finance system, accounting for only 2.2 percent of total state tax revenue. The importance of the tax is unlikely to increase. Personal and intangible property taxes are highly unpopular and difficult to administer. The one area that may allow for revenue growth is the taxation of real property. The pressures on business, consumption, and even personal income taxes may leave states no other choice but to rely more heavily on real property taxes. Given the reforms that have taken place over the past quarter-century, statewide property taxes will likely be considered politically acceptable to lawmakers.

Wealth Transfer Taxes

States tax transfers of wealth by imposing levies on gifts, inheritances, and estates. State tax revenues coming from transfers of wealth account for less than 1 percent of total state tax revenue and make up an even smaller percentage of total state revenue. All of the states combined collected just over $6 billion in estate, inheritance, and gift taxes in 1998.

The issue of whether states should tax wealth transfers either at the time of death or through gifts has been hotly debated for two decades. In many respects, the debate at the state level has paralleled a similar debate in Congress. Those who believe that the state governments should refrain from taxing wealth transfers have plainly been winning the argument. The overwhelming trend over the past quarter-century has been to eliminate or sharply reduce the reliance on state inheritance, estate, and gift taxes.

Opponents of the tax claim that it discourages saving and inhibits capital formation; they argue that it is little more than a manifestation of the politics of envy (Brunori 2000b). Politicians decry the estate tax as "confiscatory"—a term that could actually apply to any tax. One of the most compelling arguments against the tax is that it is unfair to those who own small businesses or family farms.

Those who support the federal estate tax cite its progressivity. Because only the wealthiest 2 percent of the population ever pay the federal tax, it closely adheres to the concept of ability to pay. The estate tax also captures income (in the form of appreciated assets) that would otherwise go untaxed. There are also less-sophisticated arguments based on the evils of inherited wealth. Those who inherit substantial wealth, this line of thinking goes, might not be productive members of society.

Supporters and opponents have some views in common. Both sides agree that people spend far too much money trying to avoid the tax, although they disagree about whether that spending reflects excessive rates or too many loopholes. Both sides agree that the federal estate tax does not result in much revenue, at least compared with other taxes. Opponents say this lack of revenue justifies eliminating the tax, while supporters say it demonstrates the need to strengthen the tax.

The debate over wealth transfer taxes has never risen to the same level of intensity in the states as it has at the federal level. Most people—except for tax lawyers—are barely aware of how, or whether, their state imposes a tax at death (Brunori 2000b).

Unlike the federal government, states impose two types of taxes at the time of death. First, all states impose an estate tax. An estate tax is a levy on the privilege of transferring property at death, measured by the value of the estate. In every state, the estate tax is designed to be absorbed by the credit allowed under the federal estate tax for state death taxes. A person subject to federal estate tax receives a credit for state estate taxes up to a certain amount. Most states impose their estate taxes at rates that ensure that the entire amount will be credited against the federal tax bill. Indeed, the majority of states match their estate taxes to the federal estate tax credit. The estate tax credit system is thus little more than an intergovernmental transfer of funds. Because the federal estate tax excludes the first $650,000 of assets (and all transfers to spouses), 98 percent of Americans are not subject to the tax. The people who do not pay federal estate taxes, by and large, do not pay state estate taxes either. As the federal estate tax exclusion continues to increase (it is scheduled to reach $1 million by 2006), even fewer people will be subject to the tax.

The second type of levy imposed by the states at the time of death is the inheritance tax. An inheritance tax is levied on the privilege of receiving property from a deceased relative. Unlike estate taxes, inheritance taxes are not designed to be absorbed by the credit available under the federal estate tax. Inheritance taxes are imposed independent of federal estate tax liability. Inheritance taxes are much more problematic for the state, because they increase the tax liability of its citizens. Moreover, poor and middle-income people often have to pay the tax. The burdens associated with the inheritance tax have led to its repeal in many states. Indeed, since 1980, 20 states have abolished or partially abolished their inheritance tax levies. And the pressure to repeal the tax continues to be felt in most of the 14 states still collecting the tax (Brunori 2000b).

Gift taxes are even more rare. In 1980, 14 states imposed gift taxes under circumstances similar to federal gift taxation. By 2000, only four states (Connecticut, Louisiana, North Carolina, and Tennessee) imposed taxes on gifts. The political unpopularity and the costs of administration make gift taxation extremely impractical for the states.

Although wealth transfer taxes could add a measure of progressivity to state tax systems, they are unlikely to become a more important source of revenue. Estate/pick-up tax revenue will continue to fall as federal estate tax exclusions increase. Other types of wealth transfer taxes are likely to be repealed altogether.

NOTES

1. For example, according to its Web site, the South Carolina Department of Revenue administers 32 different types of taxes (http://www.sctax.org). The West Virginia Department of Taxation administers 28 different taxes and a large number of fees (http://wv.us/taxdiv). These examples are typical of most states.

2. All state tax and other revenue data are for 1998 and are from the U.S. Census Bureau (2000).

3. There are numerous products upon which an excise is levied. See, for example, Rafool (1998). A description of how each of these taxes operates is beyond the scope of this work.

4. All states except Alaska and Hawaii participate in the International Fuel Tax Agreement, which allows interstate carriers to report their tax liability to one state. The fuel tax is then allocated based on miles traveled.

5. One alternative to taxing products known to be harmful would be to ban such products from the marketplace. But, as experience has shown, prohibition has not been very successful in the United States.

6. Automobiles' increased fuel efficiency and the declining rate of smokers have also contributed to the decline of excise tax yields.

7. Real property taxes account for about 75 percent of local government revenue (U.S. Census Bureau [2000]). The percentage is high despite many political and legal obstacles (Youngman 1998).

8. Because of the vast administrative difficulties, virtually no states still tax *intangible* personal property.

REFERENCES

Brunori, David. 2000a. "A Tax Cut Worth Making: Cutting Fuel Taxes." *State Tax Notes* (March 13): 829–831.

———. 2000b. "Taxing Death, and Other Happy Thoughts." *State Tax Notes* (April 17): 1369–1371.

———. 1999. "Taxing Sin: The Assault on Tobacco Continues." *State Tax Notes* (April 9): 1321–1322.

Chernick, Howard, and Andrew Reschovsky. 2000. "Yes! Consumption Taxes Are Regressive." *State Tax Notes* (October 12): 1023–1033.

Ebel, Robert, and Therese J. McGuire, eds. 1986. "Final Report of the Minnesota Tax Study Commission." *Staff Papers*. St. Paul, Minn.: Butterworths Legal Publishers.

Governor's Commission on Fair Taxation. 1999. "1999 State Tax Collections by State." Charleston, W.Va.: Department of Tax and Revenue. Http://www.taxdmin.org/fta/rate.

Mackey, Scott, and Mandy Rafool. 1998. "State and Local Value-Based Taxes on Motor Vehicles." *State Tax Notes* (February 16): 541–545.

Rafool, Mandy. 1998. "State Tourism Taxes." *State Tax Notes* (March 23): 909–941.

Streitfeld, David. 2000. "States Go after Revenue from Online Tobacco Sales." *Washington Post*, August 29, 1.

U.S. Census Bureau. 2000. "Federal, State, and Local Governments: 1998 State Government Finance Data." Http://www.census.gov/govs/www/state98.html.

Youngman, Joan. 1998. "Property, Taxes, and the Future of Property Taxes." In *The Future of State Taxation*, edited by David Brunori (111–128). Washington, D.C.: Urban Institute Press.

9

Other Sources of State Revenue

I can't believe that people will keep losing property to such an extent that it will continue to make us money.

—Legislator commenting on his state's
claims to abandoned property

States do not rely on taxes for all revenue. In 1998, state governments only raised 43.2 percent of their total revenue from taxes.[1] The rest of their revenue comes from a variety of sources, including direct payments from the federal government, user fees, service charges, licensing, and lottery and gambling proceeds. Increasingly, states have also raised revenue through litigation; the most recent example of such litigation is the multibillion-dollar settlement of lawsuits against the tobacco industry. In addition, states have raised revenue by seizing unclaimed or abandoned property.[2]

Many of these sources of revenue are administered and imposed in a way similar to state taxes. They all require individuals and businesses connected to the state to pay money to the state government in return for specific services or benefits (e.g., the use of state parks, authorization to operate a motor vehicle, or a license to practice in a regulated profession).

Charges, fees, licenses, and lotteries differ from taxes in that they do not apply to the general public. For example, while income taxes generally apply to anyone with taxable income, license fees are charged only to individuals seeking to practice law, medicine, accounting, or some other regulated profession. The distinction between fees and taxes is important because many statutory and constitutional rules govern states' authority to tax, which is not the case with fees. The laws of the state usually dictate types of taxes, bases, and administrative requirements. Moreover, limitations on states' power to tax, always a pressing concern in this age of antitax politics, do not generally apply to fees and charges.

Intergovernmental aid, litigation awards, and unclaimed property differ more significantly from traditional taxes. These revenue sources are not necessarily collected from individuals living or firms conducting business in the state. Nor are they necessarily collected from people or firms that benefit from state services. One of the great political motivations for collecting these types of nontax revenue is that they often are paid by nonresidents.

The use of these nontax sources of revenue has grown significantly over the past decade. In the aggregate, the states raised $274 billion from nontax sources in 1995. That amount increased by 14 percent to approximately $313 billion in 1998. These nontax sources constitute a large portion of virtually every state's budget, with more than 50 percent of every dollar spent by state governments coming from nontax sources. Thus, the public services provided by the states depend to a large extent on nontax revenue.

Nontax sources of revenue are likely to continue to grow in relative importance, though more slowly than in the past. As discussed in previous chapters, traditional sources of state tax revenue are being seriously challenged by political, technological, and economic developments, such as the growth of electronic commerce and expanding global trade.

Policy Issues Presented by Nontax Revenue

To the extent that state governments can raise revenue from indirect methods such as intergovernmental aid, licenses, and unclaimed property, many states may feel less pressure to address the problems that continue to plague virtually every type of tax. Strengthening sales and business taxes requires large-scale reforms that will generate significant political debate and controversy. In the short run, the use of nontax revenue to offset a declining tax base may allow policymakers to postpone facing the political maelstrom of tax reform.

But the failure to develop sound tax systems will result in long-term problems for state fiscal systems. Despite the importance of nontax revenue, there are inherent limitations to the growth of virtually all types of nontax revenue. And such sources of revenue cannot be relied upon to finance substantially more public services than they do currently.

Besides providing policymakers with a way to temporarily address current fiscal challenges, reliance on nontax revenue is troubling for several other reasons. First, the burden of paying for these revenues falls on taxpayers who do not live in the state and thus do not have a stake in the financial security or public policies of the state. As discussed in chapter 4, exporting the burdens of paying for public services has been a very attractive option for lawmakers. At some level, state tourists, consumers, and businesses will refrain from doing business in a state with an overly aggressive taxation system. Those same considerations do not generally exist with the exportation of nontax obligations. State lawmakers may relish the thought of spending money obtained from the federal government from state tobacco companies, or from persons or businesses who have lost or abandoned property in the state. Using nontax sources of revenue is more palatable than raising constituents' taxes.

Because the money is not coming from the pockets of the citizens, this political bias may seem natural. But the policy ramifications for relying too heavily on nontax revenue to fund public services are significant. For example, lawmakers in states that rely heavily on nontax revenue will feel less pressure to be accountable to the citizens when spending that revenue. Because the citizens are not asked to bear a burden equal to costs, states are likely to expand services beyond the tax capacity of the citizens. This tendency could give rise to charges that policymakers are looking for a convenient way to expand the scope and size of state government.

Moreover, since the citizens are not paying the full costs of services, state spending is more likely to be ineffective. Political leaders are less likely to be accountable to out-of-state providers of nontax revenue than to the taxpayers who vote. Although it is true that citizens have not generally held legislators responsible for spending decisions, raising revenue from nontax sources makes such accountability even less likely.

Finally, democratic principles require that those who benefit from government policies be responsible for payment of these services. Only if citizens are required to bear the burden of paying for services will they take part in the decisions that government makes. Declining voter turnout in the United States has been partly attributed to the electorate's feeling that it has no stake in government policy. Using nontax revenue to finance services can only add to those feelings of detachment.

While nontax revenue will continue to grow in the near future, it is incapable of sustained growth. Most of the sources of nontax revenue are—in the long run—incapable of growing to meet spending needs. The number of services for which user fees or charges can be levied is limited. The state cannot charge fees for services generally available to all citizens. And without a dramatic shift in policy, states cannot charge fees for services that are fundamental to good government, such as police protection. Lottery and other gambling operations have begun to face serious political opposition in some states, and the growth in gambling revenue has apparently leveled off. The percentage of total revenue collected from unclaimed property is also unlikely to increase.

Moreover, many types of nontax revenue are unpredictable. Intergovernmental aid, for example, is dependent on federal policy and congressional appropriation. As numerous scholars have noted, the levels and types of funding to the states have changed from administration to administration for much of the last half-century (Conlan 1998).

Finally, many sources of nontax revenue pose serious equity problems. User fees, charges, and especially state lotteries are decidedly regressive. Low-income citizens spend a greater percentage of their income on these nontax charges. These types of revenue-raising policies only worsen the plight of poor and middle-class citizens.

For these reasons, state government spending of nontax revenue may come under increased scrutiny in the press and by citizen groups. Until such time, however, the majority of revenue spent by the states will be collected from nontax sources. The major types of nontax revenue sources and some of the policy problems associated with each are discussed below.

Intergovernmental Aid

The United States government contributes $240 billion a year to the states. Federal aid constituted about 22 percent of the total state revenue in 1998, and was rivaled only by sales and personal income taxes in importance. Federal monies are primarily provided to fund congressionally mandated programs or to further policies that serve national interests. Most of the federal funds are provided to pay for mandated public safety projects and for Medicaid, Temporary Assistance for Needy

Families, and other wealth-transfer payments administered by the states. In most cases, the revenue simply reimburses the states for the costs of administering the programs. Without this reimbursement, most states would not undertake certain projects.

In this regard, the amount of federal funds received by states is deceiving. State governments do not generally have discretion to spend federal monies as they wish. Thus, aid received from the federal government leads to a loss of state control over the underlying policy program. Federal funding is almost always payment for mandates issued by the federal government. The monies are rarely available to be used by the states at their discretion.

Another drawback, as noted above, is that the federal payments are often unpredictable. Federal policy often changes with administrations, and the amount of money received from the federal government often varies over time. The academic literature on fiscal federalism has detailed the wide variances in federal policies of providing aid to the states and for paying for mandated programs (Conlan 1998).

In some instances, the states are granted federal funds to further national programs, but are left to decide how best to use the money. The welfare reform of the late 1990s is a recent example. The welfare programs under Aid to Families with Dependent Children were transformed from individual entitlements to capped block grants. Under the previous law, the federal government matched the states dollar for dollar for money spent on welfare. The reforms removed the incentive for the states to increase welfare spending.

When the states do have discretion, funds may be spent on programs or policies that have little to do with the intended federal purpose. For example, New York received more than $1 billion from the federal government for antipoverty programs in 1999. Instead of paying for the antipoverty programs, however, the state used the money to indirectly fund tax cuts. Rather than increasing the number of programs to help the poor, the state decided to treat the federal money as surplus cash (Brunori 2000). Similarly, federal monies in Texas ($162 million), Minnesota ($100 million), Connecticut ($48 million), and Michigan ($120 million) all went to pay for social service programs that the states had once paid for themselves. Those states decided to gave tax cuts and rebates (in some cases, very large cuts and rebates) to residents rather than use the money to increase social service spending.

Lotteries/Gambling

At 1 percent of total state revenues, gambling revenues are a small but important source of revenue for specific state services, with lotteries generating the largest source of gambling revenue. Revenue raised from state-run lotteries totaled $12.1 billion in 1998, or just over 1 percent of total state revenue. As of 2000, 37 states and the District of Columbia operated lotteries.[3] New York State raised the most revenue from its lottery operations, collecting over $1.5 billion in 1998. Of the states operating lotteries, South Dakota raised the least revenue, collecting only $5.8 million in 1998 (Chervin 1999).

States generally operate the lotteries and keep all of the net proceeds. Out of 38 jurisdictions, 10 (including the District of Columbia) used the net revenues from lotteries exclusively for general funds. Sixteen states earmarked all or part of the revenue for education; the rest was earmarked for a variety of other uses (Clotfelter et al. 1999). Because some portion of lottery revenue in most states is allotted to education spending, significant political and public support exists for lotteries.

Lotteries are not the only types of gambling sanctioned by state governments. Many states have allowed citizens to wager on horse racing, dog racing, and jai alai for years. States have increasingly turned to casino gambling as a source of revenue. For years, only Nevada allowed casino gambling; in 1976, New Jersey decided to allow it as well. By 1999, at least 13 states allowed some form of casino gambling. This figure does not include the 16 states that allow casino gambling on Indian reservations. Video poker and slot machines are also legal in many states. But these other types of gambling activities raise only a small amount of revenue for the states. Nevada, which boasts the most significant legalized gambling operations in the country, raises about a quarter of its revenue from gambling (Gold 1993). No other state raises close to 0.5 percent of its revenue from gambling.

GAMBLING POLICY ISSUES. While the revenue from gambling has continued to grow, so too has the controversy over using it to fund public services. By all measures, gambling and particularly lotteries are regressive (Sullivan 2000). The poor and the middle class pay a far higher percentage of their annual income for gambling than do wealthy individuals. Families with yearly incomes below $10,000 average $597 of lottery purchases annually, or about 6 percent of their income. Families with incomes above $100,000 average $289 in lottery purchases, or about 0.3 percent of their income (Clotfelter et al. 1999). State governments that operate lotteries profit at the expense of the poor. Despite the evidence, policymakers in 37 states and the District of Columbia have chosen this regressive method of raising revenue.

Moreover, gambling can be addictive. From a policy standpoint, the risk that residents will become addicted to state-sponsored gambling is a serious pitfall of legalized gambling. On these grounds, gambling has routinely been criticized as an unsound policy choice (Brunori 2000; Gold 1993; Sullivan 2000).

Proponents argue that allowing the state to run and regulate gambling is a better option than having organized crime do so. An important difference between state-run and mob-run gambling is that the state government can reach many more people through extensive advertising campaigns. Invitations to gamble in one- or two-dollar increments are ubiquitous (appearing on television, in newspapers, and at virtually every convenience and grocery store). While the majority of citizens in many states support lotteries, gambling offends a sizable segment of society. Many people find gambling, whether legally sanctioned or not, immoral and unethical. These individuals question whether the state should be promoting a morally questionable activity as a means of paying for government.

For many of these reasons, there is a growing movement to scale back gambling in the states. In 2000, proposals to legalize or expand existing gambling operations in Arkansas, South Carolina, Georgia, Maine, South Dakota, and West Virginia met with serious opposition (Jefferson 2000). Those taking the lead in opposing gambling have included religious and civic organizations, as well as civil rights groups such as the NAACP (Manuel 2000).

But the pressure to raise money to pay for government services gives those in favor of legalized gambling a powerful argument. In most states, gambling advocates have turned the question from the morality of gambling to the use of gambling revenue to pay for politically attractive programs. In most states, lottery proceeds are earmarked for either education spending or assistance to the elderly. Those who would curb lottery activity must overcome the charge that a change in policy would hurt funding for schools and seniors.

User Fees, Licenses, Service Charges

Traditionally, local governments used fees and charges much more than any other level of government. This was due mainly to the fact that many local government services were particularly adaptable to a fee-based system of finance. Moreover, in recent years, limitations on local governments' ability to impose property taxes have led to greater use of fees and charges (Dresch and Sheffrin 1997).

Increasingly, however, state governments have adopted a wide range of fees, licenses, and charges to supplement their general budgets. In 1999, user fees, charges, and licenses accounted for nearly 6.9 percent of total state revenue and exceeded $76 billion, compared with $64.7 billion in 1995.

Once again, the rapid growth of fees and charges has been fueled in part by limitations on existing tax systems. States turn to user fees, licenses, and charges when raising additional revenue from consumption and income taxes is impossible for political or economic reasons. But the growth in user fees and charges is also attributable to the public's acceptance of the benefits theory of taxation; in other words, fees and charges are acceptable because only those who use the service pay the fee.

During the 1990s, states imposed fees and charges on a wide variety of public services. States collect the most revenue for tuition for public higher education and charges for public health care. But states also charge fees for a myriad of other services, including access to state parks and recreation centers, waste disposal, and highway tolls. The state also earns revenue from granting licenses. Most state-regulated professionals (lawyers, doctors, dentists, accountants, morticians, veterinarians, and many others) require a license from the state. The licenses purportedly defray the costs of regulating the profession. The states, of course, also grant licenses to operate motor vehicles.

Policymakers will need to address two primary problems related to user fees, licenses, and charges in the coming years. First, fees and charges tend to be regressive. For most government services that entail a fee or charge, the poor are burdened to a much greater extent than the wealthy. For virtually all such fees, lower-income citizens spend proportionately more than wealthier citizens.

Supporters of fees and licenses argue that because user fees and licenses are essentially based on consumption choices, the equity problems are minimized. After all, no one is forced to visit a state park and pay the entrance fee. Similarly, no one is forced to work in a profession in which a license is required. And, in fact, the poor are probably less likely to visit state parks (or engage in other fee-based activities) than the wealthy. That, of course, renders the public services for which states charge fees available primarily to the wealthier citizens of the state. Few would argue that government should provide services only to those who can afford to pay. By charging a fee, the states effectively prevent part of their populations from receiving the services. Moreover, because most fees do not cover the costs of providing the benefit, those using fee-based government services (e.g., wealthier citizens) effectively receive a subsidy.

Second, the number of services for which the state can charge fees is limited. Today, states impose fees on admission to parks and museums, tuition for higher education, and tolls on access to roads, bridges, and tunnels. A variety of professionals (barbers, lawyers, accountants, morticians, etc.) are required to obtain—and pay for—licenses. But few items are left that can be subject to user fees and few additional professions can require government regulation. Only those professions that, if unregulated, pose serious financial, health, or public safety risks can justifiably be licensed. User fees and charges cannot be levied on public safety and public health services. And for administrative reasons, they cannot be charged for services that are easily available to wide segments of society.

Finally, fees and licenses are levied on a per transaction basis. Citizens using state services pay a flat fee; citizens desiring to practice in a regulated profession pay flat license fees. Like most excise taxes, fees and license revenue do not grow with inflation. Thus, unless the legislature raises the fees and license amounts, these sources of revenue will decline as a percentage of total revenue as inflation rises.

But raising fees and licenses is subject to inherent limitations. Rapidly increasing fees will decrease the number of people using the service, especially for discretionary services such as public parks. Tuition increases will cause students to consider attending other institutions of higher learning. And at some point the number of people applying for professional licenses will decline if the licenses become too expensive. Of course, besides having to take market conditions into account, political leaders are naturally wary of increasing the costs of public education, tolls, park access, motor vehicle licenses, and other services demanded by their constituents.

LITIGATION ACTIVITIES. Another source of nontax revenue comes from litigation activities. States have filed lawsuits against large corporations that have allegedly harmed the interests of the states' citizens. In at least one case, this strategy has proved very successful.

These litigation activities are justified by the states as a means of recovering funds lost on account of negligent, tortious, and even criminal behavior on the part of large corporations. The monies may have been lost directly by individuals and businesses. But more commonly, the state is seeking redress for the inappropriate or illegal behavior's costs to the government.

To date, the most lucrative example of this new source of revenue has been the well-publicized lawsuit against the tobacco industry. In 1994, Mississippi filed suit against the five largest tobacco companies, alleging that the companies conspired to manufacture a product (cigarettes) that was known to be hazardous to the health of users. That is, the state asserted that the companies knew that cigarettes, if used as intended, caused significant health risks. Mississippi sought reimbursement for the substantial amount of money spent on smoking-related medical costs. Thereafter, every state filed similar suits against the tobacco companies.

The tobacco companies settled lawsuits with Mississippi, Texas, Florida, and Minnesota, and agreed to pay these states a total of $40 billion. In 1998, the tobacco companies reached a settlement with the 46 other states, in which the companies agreed to pay the states a total of $206 billion over a 25-year period. It was agreed that the money would be disbursed, starting in January 2000, according to a formula agreed to by the parties. Under that formula, California and New York would receive the most money—more than $25 billion each. Wyoming was slated to receive the least—about $486 million.

Some states earmarked part of the revenue for smoking-cessation programs, while others earmarked some of the money for health programs to assist those afflicted with smoking-related diseases. But most of the money will be spent at the discretion of the state legislatures (Brunori 2000). The tobacco settlement will be used to pay for transportation, education, pay raises, and other programs that governments typically use tax revenue to fund. Illinois and Connecticut provided tax cuts with the tobacco money (Brunori 2000).

The awards from tobacco litigation have provided states the opportunity to look for other alleged wrongdoers. Many states have considered bringing legal action against gun manufacturers to recoup some of the money spent as a result of gun violence. While states generally have legitimate claims against the corporations, litigation activities are not a viable revenue producer. Certainly, states cannot make budget forecasts on the basis of damages that might be collected from lawsuits, and litigation itself requires a huge amount of resources. Moreover, raising revenue through litigation opens the government up to charges that it is bypassing the legislative process.

Unclaimed Property

In addition to the increased litigation activities, states have sought other nontax sources of revenue. In the late 1990s, states turned to stricter enforcement of pre-existing escheat laws as a source of revenue. Statutory authority allows unclaimed property to be seized by the state under certain circumstances.[4] Unclaimed property is generally defined as property held and owed to another for a specified period of time and without the other's exercise of a right of ownership.

Examples of unclaimed property that may be seized by the state are bank accounts, security deposits, stock certificates, dividend checks, gift certificates, and other financial assets. The most common type of unclaimed property sought by the states is health care overpayments. Overpayment of health care costs by Medicare, Medicaid, and private insurance is common. Hospitals and other health care providers traditionally credited the account of the patient. But because most of the credit goes unclaimed, the hospital keeps the money.

States have increasingly begun to audit corporations to seize unclaimed property, and such audits have become more aggressive (Fiore 1999). Many practitioners have noted that unclaimed property audits have become an important part of state tax practice (Boucher, Hall, and Chenowth 1999). Few data are available on the total amount of unclaimed property seized by the states. But given the attention the subject has received both from practitioners and the government, the amounts could be substantial (Houghton 1999).

Nonetheless, unclaimed property is clearly not a significant part of the overall state fiscal system. And relying on unclaimed property is not likely to become a significant source of revenue for the states.

NOTES

1. All state tax and revenue data are from the U.S. Census Bureau (2000).
2. This chapter does not attempt to cover all sources of nontax revenue. For example, some states raise revenue through royalty payments and using state-run liquor stores. Only sources that have resulted in significant policy discussions are described here.
3. According to U.S. Census Bureau data, Alabama, Alaska, Arkansas, Hawaii, Mississippi, Nevada, North Carolina, North Dakota, Oklahoma, South Carolina, Tennessee, Utah, and Wyoming did not operate lotteries in 1998.
4. The theory behind unclaimed property seizure is that the state is in a better position to hold the property. While the original owner can make a claim to the state, the money usually stays in the possession of the government.

REFERENCES

Boucher, Karen, Noel Hall, and Matthew Chenowth. 1999. "Unclaimed Property Audits." *The Tax Advisor* (September 1): 677.
Brunori, David. 2000. "The Game of Tax Politics." *State Tax Notes* (April 26): 1517–1519.
Chervin, Stanley. 1999. "The Lure of the Lottery—Tennessee's Last Hope?" *State Tax Notes* (October 4): 913–918.
Clotfelter, Charles T., Philip J. Cook, Julie A. Edell, and Marian Moore. 1999. "State Lotteries at the Turn of the Century: Report to the National Gambling Impact Study Commission," April 23. Http://www.ngisc.gov/reports/lotfinal.pdf.
Conlan, Timothy. 1998. *From New Federalism to Devolution*. Washington, D.C.: Brookings Institution Press.
Dresch, Marla, and Steven Sheffrin. 1997. "The Role of Development Fees and Exactions in Local Public Finance." *State Tax Notes* (December 1): 1410–1447.
Fiore, Nicholas. 1999. "Unclaimed Property Audits." *Journal of Accountancy* (September 1): 104.
Gold, Steven D. 1993. "Gambling Is No Panacea for Ailing State Budgets." *State Tax Notes* (October 18): 905–909.
Houghton, Kendall. 1999. "A Primer on Unclaimed Property." *State Tax Notes* (March 8): 753–760.
Jefferson, James. 2000. "Arkansas Divided over Gambling Money and Morals Facing Nov. 7 Ballot Question on Casinos, Lottery." *Boston Globe*, October 22.
Manuel, Marlon. 2000. "Black Vote May Tilt S.C. Lottery Referendum." *Atlanta Journal Constitution*, October 25, 1.
Sullivan, Martin A. 2000. "Taxing the Sins of the Poor." *State Tax Notes* (April 17): 1377–1381.
U.S. Census Bureau. 2000. "Federal, State, and Local Governments: 1998 State Government Finance Data." Http://www.census.gov/govs/www/state98.html.

10

Policy Recommendations for State Policymakers

State tax systems were developed during a different time and for a far different economy. Political leaders drafting Wisconsin's income tax law in 1911 or Mississippi's sales tax law in 1932 could not have imagined the world today. The economy is no longer centered on manufacturing and agriculture. Products are no longer consumed near where they were made or grown. The globalization of markets and the advent of electronic commerce have revolutionized how people entertain, communicate, shop, and conduct business. The world has not witnessed economic and social change on this scale since the late 1800s.

The dramatic changes occurring throughout the economy will affect virtually all aspects of the states' tax systems. Most scholars and commentators agree that electronic commerce will be the most significant issue facing the states for many years into the 21st century.[1] If the states do not address the issues associated with electronic commerce, their revenue systems will be severely tested (Hellerstein 1998).

Globalization of the marketplace will also continue to test state tax systems. Increasingly, the ability of companies to move capital easily and to sell products and services around the world will make the compliance and administration of taxes tied to a specific state both difficult and expensive. State taxes largely depend on place. For example, income taxes are imposed on residents of or business operations within a state. Sales and use taxes (and all consumption-based excise

145

taxes) are determined by where a sale takes place or where the product or service is used. Unlike the states' tax systems, however, geographical region no longer determines how or where companies do business.

The new high-tech global economy poses two serious problems for the states. The first, and most well-documented, is the threat of declining state revenue. The sales tax (and, to a lesser extent, the corporate income tax) has continued to decrease as a percentage of state revenue. If this trend continues—and most observers think it will—the states will find themselves backed into a political corner, forced either to reduce levels of public services or to increase other types of taxes.

The states are not likely to significantly reduce services. Traditionally, most state spending has gone to public health and safety, education, and transportation. Citizens will, of course, continue to demand these basic government services. And after years of fiscal discipline, little extravagance or waste remains to be cut from most state budgets.

More likely, the states will turn to alternative sources of revenue. The most probable source of additional revenue is the personal income tax. States are limited, however, in how much they can increase the personal income tax without jeopardizing the viability and public acceptance of the tax. States may also turn to raising property and consumption taxes. But that option is also fraught with political risks, leaving the states with limited options for increasing their tax bases.

The second major problem posed by the new economy concerns state autonomy. Specifically, federal preemption of state taxing power over electronic commerce could rob states of the autonomy they exercise over their tax systems. This more esoteric problem goes to the heart of the American system of government. In the U.S. federal system, the states have always had a significant amount of sovereignty over their affairs. The question of taxing electronic commerce has been subject to considerable federal scrutiny in recent years. The growth of electronic commerce has led to a host of proposed federal legislation dealing with e-commerce tax issues. These legislative proposals have been aimed at reducing state taxing authority over electronic commerce. Some legislation has been successful. The Internet Tax Freedom Act, for example, placed a three-year "moratorium" on all new state and local taxes on electronic commerce. Other legislative proposals have sought to make that moratorium permanent (Brunori 1999c). National political leaders have also called for legislators to codify the limitations placed on state tax jurisdiction under the Supreme Court's *Quill* decision (Sheppard 2000).[2]

The most notable federal intervention in state taxation occurred in 1959 with the enactment of Public Law 86-272. This law prevents states from imposing income taxes on corporations that merely solicit orders for tangible personal property in the state. Congress has also limited state taxing authority over air travel, railroads, motor carriers, and satellite services. Electronic commerce, however, represents a far broader segment of the economy than these previous categories of federal preemption,[3] and it is likely to generate much more sales and other tax revenue. Many observers have recognized the serious implications of limiting state autonomy and the possible effects on American federalism (Brunori 2000b).

The task of addressing the problems associated with state taxation in the new economy is daunting. Solving these problems will call for unprecedented cooperation between the states, and will require wholesale reform of the revenue system in some states. Particular issues may call for further intervention by the federal government. Individual states will be unable to solve all of the problems associated with the changing world economy. They can, however, take steps to strengthen their tax systems.

The policy options described below could help states create a more efficient, equitable, and sustainable revenue structure. These policy recommendations can be implemented without significant reforms to the existing system. Most can be implemented largely without contention, cost, or delay, and can be applied to all categories of tax. These recommendations do not involve eliminating or imposing new levies. Nor do they involve altering tax burdens or tax bases. Rather, they call for policymakers and legislators to change the way they think about the tax policy process.

Know What Works

It is imperative that state policy leaders know what types of taxes and revenue structures are working and what types are not. Traditionally, however, state governments have not systematically evaluated their revenue systems. Thus, it is not surprising that many of the states' taxes and procedures, designed a half-century ago, do not work efficiently in today's economy. Legislators and policymakers are often surprised to learn of the large number of different taxes imposed by their states and that many of these taxes raise relatively paltry sums of money. Although the original reasoning behind many taxes has been lost, the taxes continue simply because "they have always been imposed."

Many states have commissioned public finance scholars to conduct in-depth studies as part of larger tax-reform efforts (Brunori 1999d; McGuire and Rio 1995). Because such studies have occurred infrequently and have usually been part of comprehensive restructuring efforts, they have typically resulted in recommendations for radical changes in the state tax laws.

To allow for more incremental improvements, legislatures or revenue departments should periodically review the state tax systems to determine if they are raising revenue in an efficient manner. Every three years, a nonpartisan, independent study should examine each tax and evaluate it on three criteria: whether it raises enough revenue to justify the administrative and compliance costs associated with its imposition; whether it hinders economic development; and whether it is capable of raising revenue in the immediate future.

Such studies would uncover taxes that raise little revenue but consume enormous administrative costs, including taxes that have been imposed for decades without economic justification. In addition, these studies would identify taxes that cannot raise revenue effectively because of new technology or shifting demographics. Such studies would also provide policymakers with information on how to strengthen existing tax bases. The results of these studies should be widely disseminated to the legislature, the media, and the public. How lawmakers ultimately respond to these periodic reviews is largely a question of political judgment. Leaders making these judgments, however, should have access to as much information as possible.

Know Where the Burdens Fall

A tax system must be fair, according to the principles of sound tax policy. Yet few states conduct incidence analyses to determine who bears the burdens or attains the benefits of proposed tax policies (Johnson and Lav 1997). Although political leaders are aware that income taxes are generally progressive and that most consumption taxes are regressive, they do not have detailed data on the relative burdens their tax systems place on the wealthy, the middle class, the poor, businesses, individuals, and nonresident entities. This lack of information has no doubt played a role in creating tax systems that are decidedly regressive. The proliferation of targeted tax incentives, extensive taxation of the incomes and estates of the working poor, and widespread use of consumption taxes are part of this legacy of ignorance.

Every state legislature should conduct an independent analysis of all tax proposals to determine which group will benefit and which group will bear the greatest burden. That information should be widely accessible to the public and press. How lawmakers react to the results of these incidence studies is again a question of political judgment. In a democratic society, however, the public should know who is paying for government—and who is not.

Consider the Experts' Opinions

Tax policies are often formulated in a way that is inconsistent with the advice or recommendations of those most knowledgeable about the subject. For example, the consensus among economists, political theorists, and public finance experts is that targeted tax incentives are an unsound method for spurring economic development. Nonetheless, targeted tax incentives have proliferated in virtually every state. Unfortunately, there are many other examples in which the advice of highly trained and experienced public finance experts goes unheard by the political leaders charged with formulating state tax policy.[4]

Legislators, of course, cannot abdicate their policy-making responsibilities. But many tax laws are proposed and supported for short-term political purposes alone. These policies may help influential industries or a leader's political allies, but they are not always in the long-term financial interest of the state. Experienced economists and public finance experts can position proposed legislation in a longer-term perspective. By soliciting qualified individuals to comment on the effects of tax policy proposals, legislators have a better chance of making the most informed decisions.

Work Together

A certain amount of competition between the states encourages innovation and efficiency. Interstate competition, however, should not preclude interstate cooperation. The immense problems plaguing tax systems—

including the taxing of electronic commerce and the proliferation of corporate tax incentives—cannot be solved by any one state. By acting alone, the states risk harmful tax competition, an ever-shrinking tax base, and the possibility of federal preemption.

The states have already laid some groundwork in the area of cooperation. Organizations such as the Federation of Tax Administrators, the National Conference of State Legislatures, and the National Governors' Association have helped states solve many problems in the past. But those efforts have succeeded only when political leaders and revenue administrators have committed to working together. Given the severity of the problems facing state taxation, that commitment to cooperation has never been more critical.

Thus far, the most effective cooperative effort has been in the area of multistate business activities. The adoption of the Multistate Tax Compact and the efforts of the Multistate Tax Commission have helped create uniform tax laws and procedures that reduce compliance burdens and minimize the possibility of double taxation. Uniformity adds a level of certainty that is essential in a sound tax system. Uniformity also benefits the states by lowering administrative costs and strengthening enforcement mechanisms. The most effective means of cooperating and achieving uniformity have been the Multistate Tax Compact and the joint efforts of the Multistate Tax Commission. No organization has done more to help to make state tax systems fair and efficient as they apply to interstate and international commerce. At the same time, the Commission has successfully protected state fiscal authority.

Strive for Sound Tax Policy

The ultimate goal of these recommendations is to create sound tax policy. To arrive at that goal, policymakers and political leaders should demand a tax system with stability, where the rules of the game rarely change. Leaders should demand diverse revenue sources to end undue reliance on any one particular tax. They should demand a broad tax base—one with a minimum of exemptions, deductions, credits, and other loopholes. Broadening the tax base will allow a state to maintain lower tax rates for everyone.

Those formulating state tax policy should work toward a system that ensures fairness, one that shields the poorest and ensures that all households earning the same amount of income pay the same amount of tax. Legislators should devise a system that is easy to understand and inexpensive in terms of compliance and administration. And they should work toward a system that minimizes interstate tax competition and business tax incentives.

These recommendations repeat the principles of sound tax policy discussed in chapter 2. While difficult to attain, these principles are an important roadmap for policymakers. Adhering to the principles will result in a fairer, more efficient, and ultimately stronger state tax system.

NOTES

1. In a series of interviews that *State Tax Notes* conducted with scholars and administrators who have had an impact on state and local taxation, the consensus was that electronic commerce was the most significant issue facing state taxation (see Brunori [1999a, 1999b, 2000a, and 2000b]).
2. State autonomy is also threatened by the dramatic growth of international trade. Many international trade agreements and treaties are thought to limit state taxing authority to some extent (Hamilton 1995).
3. For a discussion of the parallel between federal preemption and recent federal legislative efforts to limit state taxing authority over electronic commerce, see Mines (1997).
4. A review of news stories in *State Tax Notes* and the general press on tax proposals between 1996 and 1999 reveals that 30 percent of the proposals were enacted despite criticism from academic researchers. (Data are available from the author upon request.)

REFERENCES

Brunori, David. 1999a. "Interview: FTA's Harley Duncan on the MTC, Cooperation, E-Commerce." *State Tax Notes* (October 18): 1037–1041.

———. 1999b. "Interview: CBPP's Lav on Fairness, Progressivity, and the Net." *State Tax Notes* (October 25): 1103–1108.

———. 1999c. "Starting to Slide Down the Slippery Slope: What's Next for the Internet Tax Freedom Act?" *State Tax Notes* (February 22): 577–579.

———. 1999d. "Another Reform Commission Reports: Will Anyone Listen?" *State Tax Notes* (June 14): 1973–1975.

———. 2000a. "Interview: Robert P. Strauss on State-Local Tax Policy, Reform." *State Tax Notes* (June 26): 2153–2155.

———. 2000b. "Interview: Dan Bucks of the Multistate Tax Commission." *State Tax Notes* (July 31): 303–309.

Hamilton, Amy. 1995. "NCSL Panelists Discuss State Sovereignty in International Trade Agreements." *State Tax Notes* (July 9): 251.

Hellerstein, Walter. 1998. "Electronic Commerce and the Future of State Taxation." In *The Future of State Taxation*, edited by David Brunori (207–223). Washington, D.C.: Urban Institute Press.

Johnson, Nicholas, and Iris Lav. 1997. "Are State Taxes Becoming More Regressive?" *State Tax Notes* (October 6): 893.

McGuire, Therese, and Jessica Rio. 1995. "Toward State Tax Reform: Lesson from State Tax Studies." Paper prepared for The Finance Project. Http://www. financeproject.org/toward.html.

Mines, Paull. 1997. "Conversing with Professor Hellerstein." *Tax Law Review* 52: 581.

Sheppard, Doug. 2000. "U.S. Senators Propose to Codify Nexus Standards for Sales, Income Taxes." *State Tax Notes* (April 17): 1364–1365.

Index

About the Author

David Brunori is a journalist, author, educator, and lawyer who specializes in tax and government issues. He is a frequent speaker at conferences around the United States on the subject of state and local tax policy. Brunori is contributing editor for *State Tax Notes* magazine and the author of *The Politics of State Taxation*, a weekly column focusing on state tax and budget politics. He also teaches state and local taxation at The George Washington University Law School and George Mason University School of Law. Previously, he served as a trial attorney with the U.S. Department of Justice and practiced law with a Washington, D.C., law firm. He edited *The Future of State Taxation* (Urban Institute Press), and has published articles in the *National Tax Journal* and the *State and Local Government Review*. He earned bachelor's and master's degrees from The George Washington University and his law degree from the University of Pittsburgh School of Law.